Mnemonics For Dental Students
(MDS)

OrangeBooks Publication

Smriti Nagar, Bhilai, Chhattisgarh - 490020

Website:**www.orangebooks.in**

© Copyright, 2023, Author

First Edition, 2023

MNEMONICS FOR DENTAL STUDENTS

FIRST EDITION
VOLUME 1
FIRST YEAR BDS

DR AHMED HASAN FAROOQI T BDS

OrangeBooks Publication
www.orangebooks.in

Preface

Mnemonics mean aid in memory, which are very useful in remembering a lot of valuable points in a systematic manner.

We can remember the things in a word or sentence without consuming much space, thereby increasing the surface area of memory.

In our body systems, it is evident.

In CNS, sulci and gyri increase the surface area.

In respiratory system, alveoli increase the surface area.

In GIT, microvilli increase the surface area.

In urinary system, nephrons increase the surface area.

This book will help every dental student and pg dental entrance aspirant in their studies, which are arranged year wise subject wise and topic wise.

All the best

Contents

ANATOMY MNEMONICS

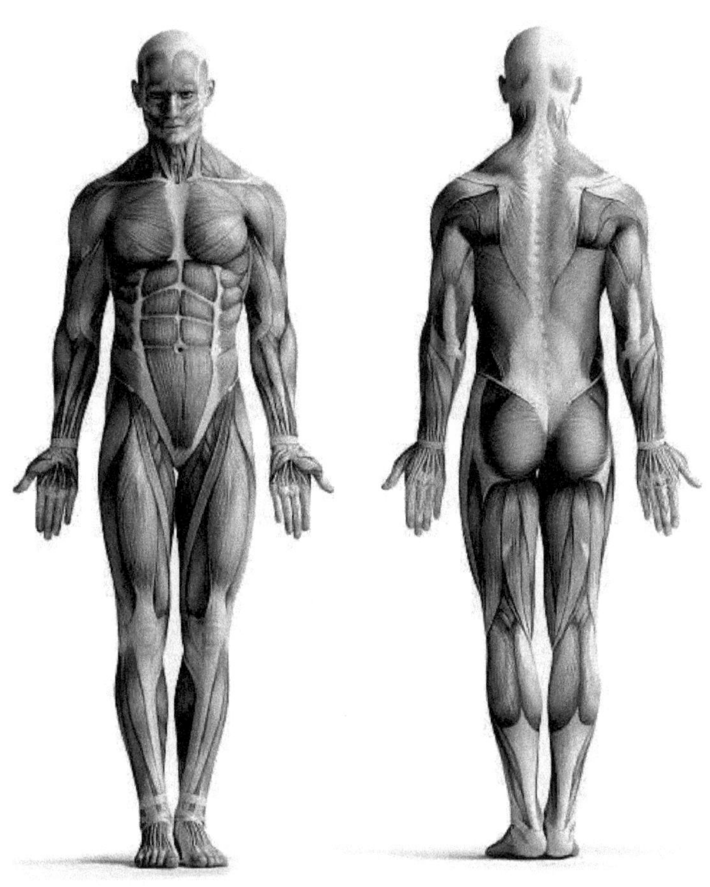

OSTEOLOGY

BONES OF SKULL : TT / Tw Tw

- Twenty Two In Number

CALVARIA / BRAIN CASE : 8 BONES

PAIRED : PTP

- Parietal

- Temporal

FACIAL SKELETON : 14 ALPHABETS : F → F

- Forteen Bones

UNPAIRED BONES : MUV

- Mandible

- Vomer

EXTERIOR OF THE SKULL : NORMA VERTICALIS

SUTURES : CSLM

- Coronal Suture

- Sagittal Suture

- Lambdoid Suture

- Metopic Suture

PTERION : PTS F

- Parietal

- Temporal

- Sphenoid

- Frontal

DEEP TO PTERION : MAMS

- Middle Meningeal Vein

- Anterior Division of Middle Meningeal Artery

- Stem of The Lateral Sulcus Of Brain

MEDIAL PTERYGOID PLATE : ATTACHMENTS : PSAP

- Pharyngobasilar fascia

- Superior Constrictor

- Auditory Tube

- Pterygomandibular Raphe

LATERAL PTERYGOID PLATE : ATTACHMENTS :

- Lateral Surface : LLL : gives origin to Lower Head of Lateral Pterygoid Muscle

- Medial Surface : MDMP : gives origin to Deep head of Medial Pterygoid

INCISIVE FORAMEN : TRANSMITS : ING

- Nasopalatine Nerve (Terminal Part)
- Greater Palatine Vessels (Terminal Parts)

GREATER PALATINE FORAMEN : TRANSMITS : GAG

- Anterior Palatine Nerve
- Greater Palatine Vessels

FORAMEN OVALE : TRANSMITS : MALE

- Mandibular Nerve
- Accessory Meningeal Artery
- Lesser Petrosal Nerve
- Emissary Vein

FORAMEN SPINOSUM : TRANSMITS : MMM

- Middle Meningeal Artery
- Meningeal Branch of Mandibular Nerve / Nervus Spinosus
- Middle Meningeal Vein (Posterior Trunk)

FORAMEN MAGNUM : TRANSMITS
Through Wider Posterior Part : MM

- Medulla Oblongata (Lowest Part)
- Meninges – Three

Through Subarachnoid Space : SVSS

- Spinal Accessory Nerves

- Vertebral Arteries

- Sympathetic Plexus around Vertebral Arteries

- Spinal Arteries (Posterior)

- Spinal Artery (Anterior)

Through Narrow Anterior Part : AVM

- Apical Ligament of Dens

- Vertical brand of Cruciate Ligament

- Membrana Tectoria

HYPOGLOSSAL OR ANTERIOR CONDYLAR CANAL : TRANSMITS : HEMA

- Hypoglossal Nerve

- Meningeal Branch of Hypoglossal Nerve

- Emissary Vein connecting Sigmoid sinus with Internal jugular vein (ESI)

- Meningeal Branch of Ascending Pharyngeal Artery (MAP)

POSTERIOR CONDYLAR CANAL : TRANSMITS : PESS / POSESS

- Emissary vein connecting Sigmoid sinus with Suboccipital venous plexus (ESS)

JUGULAR FORAMEN : TRANSMITS

Through The Anterior Part : IPS MAP

- Inferior Petrosal Sinus
- Meningeal Branch of Ascending Pharyngeal Artery

Through The Middle Part : IXI - IX X XI Cranial Nerves

Through The Posterior Part : IMO

- Internal Jugular Vein
- Meningeal Branch of Occipital Artery

STYLOMASTOID FORAMEN : TRANSMITS : SFP

- Facial Nerve
- Stylomastoid Branch of Posterior Auricular Artery

GANGLIA ASSOCIATED WITH FACIAL NERVE : GS Pradeep

- Geniculate : Sensory
- Submandibular and Pterygopalatine : Parasympathetic

SUBMANDIBULAR GANGLIA : SSSS

- Superior Salivatory nucleus
- Submandibular
- Sublingual

OPTIC CANAL : TRANSMITS : OOO / 3 O' s

- Optic Nerve

- Ophthalmic Artery

SUPERIOR ORBITAL FISSURE : TRANSMITS : LAT AFMS

LATeral Part : LAcrimal Nerve Trochlear Nerve

- Anastomotic branch of middle meningeal artery which anastomoses with recurrent branch of lacrimal artery

- Frontal Nerve

- Meningeal branch of Lacrimal artery

- Superior Ophthalmic Vein

Middle Part : ULNA

- Upper and Lower divisions of Occulomotor Nerve

- Nasociliary Nerve in between two divisions of occulomotor

- Abducent Nerve

Medial Part : MIS INdia

- Inferior Ophthalmic Vein

- Sympathetic Nerves from the plexus around Internal Carotid Artery

INTERNAL ACOUSTIC MEATUS : TRANSMITS : ISEL

- Seventh and Eighth Cranial Nerves

- Labrynthine Vessels

INFERIOR ORBITAL FISSURE : TRANSMITS : ZOP IC IOP

- Zygomatic Nerve

- Orbital Branches of Pterygopalatine Ganglion

- Infra orbital Nerve and Vessels

- Communication between Inferior Ophthalmic vein and Pterygoid plexus of veins

ANTERIOR ETHMOIDAL FORAMINA : TRANSMIT :

- Nerves and Vessels

[PO]STERIOR ETHMOIDAL FORAMINA : TRANSMITS : [PO]

- Only Vessels

GENIAL TUBERCLES : GGH / GG Hospital / Government General Hospital

- UPPER : gives origin to GenioGlossus

- LOWER : gives origin to GenioHyoid

SCALP, TEMPLE AND FACE

SCALP : LAYERS : SCALP

- Skin

- Connective Tissue

- Epicranial Aponeurosis

- Loose Connective Tissue

- Pericranium

OCCIPITOFRONTALIS MUSCLE : OP TF

- Occipital Belly : Posterior Auricular Branch Of Facial Nerve

- Frontal Belly : Temporal Branch Of Facial Nerve

NERVES OF SCALP AND SUPERFICIAL TEMPORAL REGION

IN FRONT OF AURICLE : SENSORY : 3 DIVISIONS OF TRIGEMINAL NERVE : OMM

- Supratrochlear and supraorbital branches of Frontal Nerve (Ophthalmic Division)

- Zygomaticotemporal branch of Zygomatic Nerve (Maxillary Division)

- Auriculotemporal Branch (Mandibular Division)

BEHIND THE AURICLE : PGA LOGON TO /
Please Go And Log On To

- Posterior division of Great Auricular Nerve (C2,C3) from Cervical Plexus - PGA

- Lesser Occipital Nerve (C2) from Cervical Plexus - LO

- Greater Occipital Nerve (C2, Dorsal Ramus) - GON

- Third Occipital Nerve (C3, Dorsal Ramus) - TO

ARTERIAL SUPPLY OF SCALP AND
SUPERFICIAL TEMPORAL REGION : SSS PO

- Supratrochlear branch of Ophthalmic Artery branch of Internal Carotid Artery

- Supraorbital branch of Ophthalmic Artery branch of Internal Carotid Artery

- Superficial Temporal Artery branch of External Carotid Artery

- Posterior Auricular Artery branch of External Carotid Artery

- Occipital Artery branch of External Carotid Artery

VENOUS DRAINAGE

- Supratrochlear and Supraorbital veins unite to form Angular Vein continues down as Facial Vein - SSAF

- Superficial Temporal Vein joins with Maxillary Vein to form Retromandibular Vein - STMR

RETROMANDIBULAR VEIN

- Anterior Division - unites with Facial to form Common Facial Vein drains into Internal Jugular Vein -A FCI

- Posterior Division - unites with Posterior Auricular Vein to form External Jugular Vein drains into Subclavian Vein - P PES

- Occipital Veins terminate in the Suboccipital Venous Plexus - OV SVP

SCALP : LYMPHATIC DRAINHAGE : APP PMO

- Anterior Part : Preauricular /Parotid

- Posterior Part : Postauricular / Mastoid and Occipital Lymph nodes

SADNESS : LLL

- Levator Labii Superioris

- Levator Anguli Oris

ANGER : ADD DNS

- Dilator Naris

- Depressor Septi

LACRIMAL APPARATUS : NCL (Non Creamy Layer) LLL

- Nasolacrimal Duct

- Conjunctival Sac

- Lacrimal Gland and its Ducts

- Lacrimal Puncta and Lacrimal Canaliculi

- Lacrimal Sac

LACRIMAL GLAND : LOP

Orbital Part : OLD

- Larger

- Deeper

Palpebral Part : SS

- Smaller

- Superficial

SIDE OF NECK

DEEP CERVICAL FASCIA (FASCIA COLLI) : CBI PPP / IP CP BP / BCI PPP

- Carotid Sheath
- Buccopharyngeal Fascia
- Investing Layer
- Pretracheal Fascia
- Prevertebral Fascia
- Pharyngobasilar Fascia

CAROTID SHEATH : CONTENTS : IC IVD / I VCD

- Internal Carotid Artery
- Common Carotid Artery
- Internal Jugular Vein
- Vagus Nerve
- Deed Cervical Lymph Nodes

SUPRASTERNAL SPACE : CONTENTS : JILS

- Jugular Venous Arch
- Interclavicular Ligament
- Lymph Node
- Sternal Heads of Right and Left Sternocleidomastoid Muscles

POSTERIOR TRIANGLE : DIVISIONS : IO LOSS

- Inferior belly of Omohyoid divides
- Larger upper part – Occipital Triangle
- Smaller lower part – Supraclavicular or Subclavian : SSS

VIRCHOW'S NODES : LSV

- Left Supraclavicular Lymph Nodes
- Scalene Nodes

TORTICOLLIS / WRY NECK : TYPES : RR CS

- Rheumatic
- Reflex
- Congenital
- Spasmodic

ANTERIOR TRIANGLE OF NECK

ANTERIOR TRIANGLE OF NECK : SUB DIVISIONS : AC MDS

- Carotid Triangle

- Muscular Triangle

- Digastric Triangle

- Submental Triangle

DIGASTRIC TRIANGLE : CONTENTS : ANTERIOR PART OF TRIANGLE STRUCTURES SUPERFICIAL TO MYLOHYOID ARE : SMS

- Superficial Part Of Submandibular Salivary Gland

- Mylohyoid Nerve And Vessels

- Submental Artery

STRUCTURES SUPERFICIAL TO HYOGLOSSUS : HIDS

- Hypoglossal Nerve

- Intermediate Tendon Of Digastric And Stylohyoid

- Submandibular Salivary Gland

POSTERIOR PART OF TRIANGLE
SUPERFICIAL STRUCTURES : SLE

- Lower Part Of Parotid gland
- External Carotid Artey

DEEP STRUCTURES : GPS / PGS

- Glossopharyngeal Nerve
- Pharyngeal Branch Of Vagus
- Part Of Parotid Gland
- Styloglossus
- Stylopharyngeus
- Styloid Process

DEEPEST STRUCTURES : II

- Internal Carotid Artery
- Internal Jugular Vein

CAROTID TRIANGLE : CONTENTS : AV NCL
ARTERIES : CIE

- Common Carotid Artery
- Internal Carotid Artery
- External Carotid Artery

VEINS : C IPL

- Common Facial Vein

- Internal Jugular Vein

- Pharyngeal Vein

- Lingual Vein

NERVES : VHSS (10, 11, 12 CRANIAL NERVES)

- Vagus Nerve, Superior Laryngeal Branch of Vagus

- Hypoglossal Nerve

- Spinal Accessory Nerve

- Sympathetic Chain

- Carotid Sheath With Its Contents

- LYMPH NODES : Deep Cervical Lymph Nodes situated along Internal Jugular Vein

EXTERNAL CAROTID ARTERY : BRANCHES : ASLO FP MS

- Ascending Pharyngeal Artery

- Superior Thyroid Artey

- Lingual Artery

- Occipital Artery

- Facial Artery

- Posterior Auricular Artery

- Maxillary Artery

- Superficial Temporal Artery

EXTERNAL CAROTID ARTERY : BRANCHES : A PMT

ANTERIOR BRANCHES : ASuLiFa

- Superior thyroid
- Lingual
- Facial

POSTERIOR BRANCHES : POP

- Occipital
- Posterior Auricular

MEDIAL BRANCHES : MAP

- Ascending Pharyngeal

[TE]RMIN[AL] BRANCHES : TMS

- Maxillary
- Superfici[AL] [TE]mpor[AL]

THYROHYOID MEMBRANE : PIERCED BY : THANSI / ANSI

- Artery : Superior Laryngeal
- Nerve : Internal Laryngeal

ANSA CERVICALIS : SSO AS SIO

- Superior Root : To Superior Belly Of Omohyoid
- Ansa Cervicalis : To Sternohyoid , Sternothyroid and Inferior Belly Of Omohyoid

PAROTID REGION

PAROTID GLAND :

PARASYMPATHETIC NERVE SUPPLY : IG TT LOG ATP

- Inferior Salivatory Nucleus
- Glossopharyngeal Nerve
- Tympanic Branch Of Glossopharyngeal Nerve
- Tympanic Plexus
- Lesser Petrosal Nerve
- Otic Ganglion
- AuriculoTemporal Nerve
- Parotid Gland

ARTERIES WITHIN THE PAROTID GLAND : TEMPO

- TEMPOral vessels
- External carotid artery
- Maxillary artery
- Posterior auricular artery

TEMPORAL AND INFRATEMPORAL REGIONS

MUSCLES OF MASTICATION : MMM MLT

- Masseter
- Medial Pterygoid
- Lateral Pterygoid
- Temporalis

LATERAL PTERYGOID : LOD

- Opens the mouth by

- Depressing the mandible

MAXILLARY ARTERY : BRANCHES

FIRST PART : Mandibular Part : DAM AI

- Deep Auricular

- Anterior Tympanic

- Middle Meningeal

- Accessory Meningeal

- Inferior Alveolar

SECOND PART : Pterygoid Part : DPM   B

- Deep Temporal

- Pterygoid

- Masseteric

- Buccal

THIRD PART : Pterygopalatine Part : PIG PAS

- Posterior Superior Alveolar

- Infraorbital

- Greater Palatine

- Pharyngeal

- Artery of Pterygoid Canal

- Sphenopalatine (Terminal Part)

TEMPOROMANDIBULAR JOINT : LIGAMENTS : LS SF (Limited Stop Fast)

- Lateral / Temporomandibular Ligament

- Sphenomandibular Ligament

- Stylomandibular Ligament

- Fibrous Capsule

MANDIBULAR NERVE : BRANCHES : FROM TRUNKS : MAP
MAIN TRUNK : MMM

- Meningeal Branch (Nervus Spinosus)

- N. to Medial Pterygoid

ANTERIOR TRUNK : AB MLT

- Buccal - Sensory

- Masseteric

- N. to Lateral Pterygoid

- Deep Temporal Nerves

POSTERIOR TRUNK : PALI / ALI

- Auriculotemporal

- Lingual

- Inferior Alveolar

CHORDA TYMPANI NERVE : CMS

- Medial to Spine of Sphenoid

AURICULOTEMPORAL NERVE : ATLAS

- Lateral Aspect of Spine of Sphenoid

SUBMANDIBULAR REGION

SUPRAHYOID MUSCLES : MDS GH

- Mylohyoid

- Digastric

- Stylohyoid

- Geniohyoid

- Hyoglossus

RELATIONS OF POSTERIOR BELLY OF DIGASTRIC

SUPERFICIAL : MASTer Piece

- MASToid process with sternocleidomastoid , splenius capitis and longissimus capitis

- Angle of mandible with medial pterygoid

- STylohyoid

- Submandibular salivary gland and lymph nodes

- Parotid gland with retromandibular vein

DEEP : Very HIT

- Vagus , accessory and hypoglossal cranial nerves

- Hyoglossus muscle

- Internal carotid, external carotid, lingual, facial and occipital arteries

- Internal jugular vein

- Transverse process of atlas with superior oblique and rectus capitis lateralis

RELATIONS OF MYLOHYOID
SUPERFICIAL : MASS

- Mylohyoid nerve and vessels
- Anterior belly of digastric
- Superficial part of submandibular salivary gland
- Submental branch of facial artery

HYOGLOSSUS : RELATIONS
SUPERFICIAL : LHS

- Lingual Nerve
- Hypoglossal Nerve
- Styloglossus
- Submandibular Ganglion
- Submandibular Gland (Deep Part)
- Submandibular Duct

DEEP : GG SLIM

- Genioglossus
- Glossopharyngeal Nerve
- Stylohyoid Ligament
- Lingual Artery
- Inferior Longitudinal Muscle of Tongue
- Middle Constrictor of Pharynx

SUBMANDIBULAR SALIVARY GLAND : SUPERFICIAL PART

RELATIONS : INFERIOR SURFACE COVERED BY : SKIN PLACE DEEP FASCIA

- Skin

- PLAtysma

- CErvical Branch of Facial Nerve

- Deep Fascia

- Facial Vein

- Submandibular Lymph Nodes

STRUCTURES IN THE NECK

THYROID GLAND

SUPERFICIAL SURFACE / LATERAL :
COVERED BY : SSSS

- Sternohyoid
- Superior Belly of Omohyoid
- Sternothyroid
- Sternocleidomastoid (Anterior Border)

MEDIAL SURFACE RELATED TO : ME TWO

- Two Tubes - Trachea and Oesophagus
- Two Muscles - Inferior Constrictor and Cricothyroid
- Two Nerves - External Laryngeal and Recurrent Laryngeal

ARTERIAL SUPPLY : ASIN / A SIN

- Superior Thyroid Artery
- Inferior Thyroid Artery

VENOUS DRAINAGE : V SUMIN

- Superior Thyroid Vein
- Middle Thyroid Vein
- Inferior Thyroid Vein

PARATHYROID GLANDS

- Superior Parathyroid : Parathyroid IV [Superior , so IV]

- Inferior Parathyroid : Parathyroid III [Inferior , so III]

SUBCLAVIAN ARTERY : BRANCHES : VIT CD

- Vertebral Artery

- Internal Thoracic Artery

Thyrocervical Trunk : ThIS Transverse / IST / TIST

- Inferior Thyroid

- Suprascapular

- Transverse Cervical

Costocervical Trunk : SDC (State Dental Council)

- Superior Intercostal

- Deep Cervical

- Dorsal Scapular Artery - Occasionally

CAROTID SHEATH : CONTENTS : COIN VAGUS MLP

- Common Carotid Artery Medially

- Internal Jugular Vein Laterally

- Vagus Between Artery and Vein Posteriorly

INTERNAL CAROTID ARTERY : PARTS : CPCC

- Cervical Part

- Petrous Part

- Cavernous Part

- Cerebral Part

SUBCLAVIAN VEIN : TRIBUTARIES : THRED

- THoracic Duct on Left Side

- Right Lymphatic Duct on Right Side

- External Jugular Vein

- Dorsal Scapular Vein

INTERNAL JUGULAR VEIN
RELATIONS : SUPERFICIAL : IPS 9 10 11 12

- Internal Carotid Artery

- Posterior Belly of Digastric

- Sternocleidomastoid

- Parotid Gland

- Superior Belly of Omohyoid

- Styloid Process

- 9, 10, 11, 12   Cranial Nerves

RELATIONS : POSTERIOR : TRAP CSF

- TRAnsverse Process of atlas

- Cervical plexus

- Scalenus anterior

- First part of subclavian artery

TRIBUTARIES : Middle CLIPS / SLIM PC

- Middle Thyroid Vein

- Common Facial Vein

- Lingual Vein

- Inferior Petrosal Sinus

- Pharyngeal Veins

- Superior Thyroid Vein

BRACHIOCEPHALIC VEIN / INNOMINATE VEIN :

RIGHT : IVF

- Internal Thoracic

- Inferior Thyroid

- Vertebral

- First Posterior Intercostal

LEFT : ABOVE + LefT

- Left Superior Intercostal

- Thymic and Pericardial Veins

STYLOID APPARATUS : SSSSS / 5 S

- III Muscles : Stylohyoid, Styloglossus, Stylopharyngeus

- II Ligaments : Stylohyoid, Stylomandibular

PREVERTEBRAL AND PARAVERTEBRAL REGIONS

SCALENE MUSCLES : MAP

- Scalenus Medius - Largest

- Scalenus Anterior

- Scalenus Posterior - Smallest

SCALENUS ANTERIOR : RELATIONS

ANTERIOR : LATE PSC

- LATEral part of carotid sheath containing internal jugular vein

- Phrenic nerve covered by prevertebral fascia

- Sternocleidomastoid

- Clavicle

POSTERIOR : BSC

- Brachial Plexus

- Subclavian Artery

- Scalenus Medius

- Cervical pleura covered by the suprapleural membrane

CERVICAL PLEXUS : BRANCHES

SUPERFICIAL (CUTANEOUS) BRANCHES : LESS GST

- LESSer Occipital (C2)

- Great Auricular (C2, C3)

- Supraclavicular (C3, C4)

- Transverse (Anterior) Cutaneous Nerve of Neck (C2, C3)

LIGAMENTS CONNECTING THE AXIS WITH THE OCCIPITAL BONE : MCA

- Membrana Tectoria

- Cruciate Ligament

- Apical Ligament Of Dens

- Alar Ligament

BACK OF THE NECK

SUBOCCIPITAL TRIANGLE : SORROO

- Rectus Capitis Posterior Major

- Rectus Capitis Posterior Minor

- Obliquus Capitis Superior (Superior Oblique)

- Obliquus Capitis Inferior   (Inferior Oblique)

SUBOCCIPITAL TRIANGLE : CONTENTS : Tax Deduction at Source

- Third part of vertebral artery

- Dorsal ramus of nerve C1 – Suboccipital nerve

- Suboccipital plexus of veins

SUBOCCIPITAL PLEXUS OF VEINS : DRAINS : Medical Officer IN Charge

- Muscular Veins

- Occipital Veins

- Internal Vertebral Venous Plexus

- Condylar Emissary Vein

CRANIAL CAVITY

CRANIAL VENOUS SINUSES

FALX CEREBRI : VENOUS SINUSES RELATED : SSS ISS SS (SS IN ALL THE 3)

- Superior Sagittal Sinus

- Inferior Sagittal Sinus

- Straight Sinus

TENTORIUM CEREBELLI : TC TS

- Transverse Sinus

- Superior Petrosal Sinus

VENOUS SINUSES : 23 IN NUMBER

- 8 (Even) Paired : $8 \times 2 = 16$

- 7 (Odd) Unpaired

- $16 + 7 = 23$

PAIRED SINUSES : PSC SIT MS

- Petrosquamous Sinus

- Sigmoid Sinus

- Cavernous Sinus

- Superior Petrosal Sinus

- Inferior Petrosal Sinus

- Transverse Sinus

- Middle Meningeal Sinus / Veins
- Sphenoparietal Sinus

UNPAIRED VENOUS SINUSES : USS IO BAP

- Superior Sagittal Sinus
- Straight Sinus
- Inferior Sagittal Sinus
- Occipital Sinus
- Basilar Plexus of Veins
- Anterior Intercavernous Sinus
- Posterior Intercavernous Sinus

CAVERNOUS SINUS : STRUCTURES IN THE LATERALL WALL : FROM ABOVE DOWNWARDS : O TOM T

- Oculomotor Nerve
- Trochlear Nerve
- Ophthalmic Nerve
- Maxillary Nerve
- Trigeminal Ganglion

STRUCTURES PASSING THROUGH THE CENTRE OF THE SINUS : I CAN

- Internal Carotid Artery
- Abducent Nerve

PITUITARY GLAND : HISTOLOGY AND HORMONES

CHROMOPHILIC CELLS

ACIDOPHILS / ALPHA CELLS : A MSC

- Mammotrophs /Prolactin Cells : Secrete Lactogenic Hormone
- Somatotrophs : Secrete Growth Hormone (STH, GH)
- Corticotrophs : Secrete ACTH

BASOPHILS / BETA CELLS : LGTB

- Luteotrophs : Secrete LH or ICSH
- Gonadotrophs : Secrete FSH
- Thyrotrophs : Secrete TSH

MIDDLE MENINGEAL ARTERY : DIVISIONS : MFP

- Frontal or Anterior Branch
- Parietal or Posterior Branch

INTERNAL CAROTID ARTERY : PARTS : IC PCC

- Cervical Part
- Petrous Part
- Cavernous Part
- Cerebral Part

PETROSAL NERVES : GREAT LED / GL ED

- Greater Petrosal Nerve : GP : Gustatory And Parasympathetic

- Lesser Petrosal Nerve : Parasympathetic

- External Petrosal Nerve : Sympathetic

- Deep Petrosal Nerve : Sympathetic

CONTENTS OF THE ORBIT

EXTRAOCULAR MUSCLES
VOLUNTARY MUSCLES : ROL

- 4 Recti : SR IR MR LR

- 2 Obliqui : SO IO

- Levator Palpebrae Superioris : LPS

INVOLUNTARY MUSCLES : SIO

- Superior Tarsal Muscle

- Inferior Tarsal Muscle

- Orbitalis

INSERTION OF RECTI MUSCLES INTO SCLERA:
AVERAGE DISTANCES OF INSERTIONS FROM THE CORNEA : SLIM
ALL ENDS IN ODD DIGIT

- Superior : 7.7 mm

- Lateral : 6.9 mm

- Inferior : 6.5 mm

- Medial : 5.5 mm

EXTRAOCULAR MUSCLES : NERVE SUPPLY
SO4 LR6 OCULOMOTOR NERVE

- SO : IV th Cranial Nerve : Trochlear Nerve

- LR : VIth Cranial Nerve : Abducent Nerve

- LPS SR : Superior Division of Oculomotor Nerve

- IR IO MR : Inferior Division of Oculomotor Nerve

ACTIONS OF INDIVIDUAL MUSCLES : O[B]LIQUE MUSCLES : A[B]DUCTION

- IO IR : Extortion

- SO SR : Intortion

- MR : Medial Rotation : Only Adduction

- LR : Lateral Rotation : Only Abduction

CILIARY GANGLION : O CL

- Lies Between Optic Nerve And Lateral Rectus

OPTIC NERVE : CROSSED SUPERIORLY BY : SON [VAN]

- Superior Ophthalmic Vein : V

- Ophthalmic Artery : A

- Nasociliary Nerve : N

CROSSED INFERIORLY BY : NMR (Nuclear Magnetic Resonance)

- Nerve to Medial Rectus

MOUTH AND PHARYNX

SOFT PALATE :MUSCLES OF SOFT PALATE : MLT PP

- Musculus Uvulae

- Levator Veli Palatini

- Tensor Veli Palatini

- Palatoglossus

- Palatopharyngeus

SOFT PALATE : BLOOD SUPPLY : GAP

- Greater Palatine Branch Of Maxillary Artery

- Ascending Palatine Branch Of Facial Artery

- Palatine Branch Of Ascending Pharyngeal Artery

TONSIL : ARTERIAL SUPPLY : MAD

- Main source - Tonsillar branch of facial artery

- Additional sources : **ADA GREAT**

- Ascending palatine branch of facial artery

- Dorsal lingual branches of lingual artery

- Ascending pharyngeal branch of external carotid artery

- GREATer palatine branch of maxillary artery

GAP BETWEEN SUPERIOR CONSTRICTOR AND SKULL BASE : SSSS

- Superior Constrictor

- Skull Base

- Semilunar

- Sinus of Morgagni

STRUCTURES PASSING THROUGH SINUS MORGAGNI : ALAP / PALA

- Auditory Tube

- Levator Veli Palatini Muscle

- Ascending Palatine Artery

- Palatine branch of ascending pharyngeal artery

GAP BETWEEN MIDDLE AND INFERIOR CONSTRICTORS : MIST

- Internal Laryngeal Nerve And

- Superior Laryngeal Vessels Pierce

- Thyrohyoid Membrane

BLOOD SUPPLY OF PHARYNX : ADA GREAT

- Ascending palatine and tonsillar branches of facial artery

- Dorsal lingual branches of lingual artery

- Ascending pharyngeal branch of external carotid artery

- GREATer palatine , pharyngeal and pterygoid branches of maxillary artery

NOSE AND PARANASAL SINUSES

KEISSELBACH'S PLEXUS : LAIN GASS

- Little's Area

- AnteroINferior Part

- Anastomoses Between

- Greater Palatine Artery

- Anterior Ethmoidal Artery

- Septal ramus of superior labial branch of facial artery

- Sphenopalatine Artery (Branch)

CONCHAE

- [S]uperior concha : [S]mallest

- [M]iddl[E] concha : [M]edial surface(projection)of [E]thmoidal labyrinth

- [IN]ferior concha : [IN]dependent bone

MIDDLE MEATUS : FEMINA H / FEHIMA

- Frontal Air Sinus Opening

- Ethmoidal Bulla

- Maxillary Air Sinus Opening

- Infundibulum

- Anterior Ethmoidal Air Sinus Opening

- Hiatus Semilunaris

PTERYGOPALATINE FOSSA : Pre Medical Test

- Pterygopalatine Ganglion

- Maxillary nerve and branches zygomatic posterior superior alveolar

- Third part of maxillary artery and its branches

PARANASAL SINUSES : ORDER OF DEVELOPMENT : MES FEE

- Maxillary Sinus

- Ethmoid Sinus

- Sphenoid Sinus

- Frontal Sinus

TONGUE

TONGUE : EXTRINSIC MUSCLES : GG HYPAS / GG HYPAST

- GenioGlossus

- HYoglossus

- PAlatoglossus

- STyloglossus

TONGUE : INTRINSIC MUSCLES : V SIT / VITS

- Verticalis

- Superior Longitudinal

- Inferior Longitudinal

- Transverse

TONGUE : PAPILLAE : FC

- Fungiform

- Filiform, Foliate

- Circumvallate

TONGUE : LYMPH VESSELS : ABC MARGINAL / MAD CENTRAL

- Apical Vessels

- Basal / Dorsal Vessels

- Central Vessels

- Marginal Vessels

BRAIN

INTRODUCTION

NEUROGLIAL CELLS : NAME OLIGODENDROCYTES

- Astrocytes

- Microglia

- Edendymal Cells

- Oligodendrocytes

PARTS OF BRAIN : PMR (Physical Medicine and Rehabilitation)

- Forebrain : Prosencephalon FP

- Midbrain : Mesencephalon MM

- Hindbrain : Rhombencephalon HR

FOREBRAIN : SUBDIVISIONS : CD

- Cerebrum (Telencephalon)

- Diencephalon (Thalamencephalon)

DIENCEPHALON : CONSISTS OF : T MESH

- Thalamus

- Metathalamus

- Epithalamus

- Subthalamus

- Hypothalamus

RHOMBENCEPHALON : CONSISTS OF : MMR

- Metencephalon

- Myelencephalon

MENINGES OF BRAIN AND CEREBROSPINAL FLUID

MENINGES : LAYERS : PAD

- Piamater

- Arachnoid

- Dura

VENTRICLE APERTURES : (M – M, L – L)

- [M]agendie foramen : [M]edial

- [L]uschka foramen : [L]ateral

CSF CIRCULATION : (C-C, A-A)

- Choroid Creates CSF

- Arachnoid granules Absorb CSF

CSF : FUNCTIONS : NCD PG

- Nourishes Nervous Tissue

- Cushion The Brain

- Decreases sudden pressure or forces on delicate nervous tissue

- Pineal gland secretions reach pituitary gland through CSF

- Glucose and oxygen to neurons constantly provided by CSF

SPINAL CORD

SPINAL CORD : GREY MATTER : SS

- Anterior Horn : Motor

- Po[s]terior Horn : [S]ensory

SPINAL CORD : SEGMENTS : CT LS

- Cervical

- Thoracic

- Lumbar

- Sacral

EXTRAPYRAMIDAL TRACTS : MR VOLT

- Medial Reticulospinal Tract

- Rubrospinal Tract

- Vestibulospinal Tract

- Olivospinal Tract

- Lateral Reticulospinal Tract

- Tectospinal Tract

ASCENDING TRACTS : FAiL or PASS

- Fasciculus Gracilis (Medially) / Tract Of Goll

- Fasciculus Cuneatus (Laterally) / Tract Of Burdach

- Anterior Spinothalamic Tract

- Lateral Spinothalamic Tract

- Posterior Or Dorsal Spinocerebellar Tract

- Anterior Spinocerebellar Tract

- Spino – Olivary Tract

- Spinotectal Tract

CRANIAL NERVES

CRANIAL NERVES : I AND II

- One Nose And Two Eyes
- Olfactory : One
- Optic : Two

CRANIAL NERVES : ATTACHED TO : 2FM 4PM

- I and II - Forebrain
- III and IV - Midbrain
- V VI VIII VIII - Pons
- IX X XI XII - Medulla

TRIGEMINAL NERVE : TOMM

- Opthalmic
- Maxillary
- Mandibular

OPHTHALMIC :
NASOCILIARY : POST LONG CILIA

- POSTerior Ethmoidal
- LONG Ciliary
- Branch to CILIAry Ganglion
- Infratrochlear
- Anterior Ethmoidal

ANTERIOR ETHMOIDAL : MAM LATE

- Middle And Anterior Ethmoidal Sinuses
- Medial Internal Nasal
- Lateral Internal Nasal
- External Nasal

MAXILLARY :

MIDDLE CRANIAL FOSSA : MM

- Meningeal Branch

PTERYGOPALATINE FOSSA : GAZYPO

- GAnglionic Branches
- Zygomatic
- Posterior Superior Alveolar

INFRAORBITAL CANAL : IMAs

- Middle superior alveolar
- Anterior superior alveolar

ON FACE : IPL NASAL

- INFRAORBITAL
- Palpebral
- Labial
- Nasal

MANDIBULAR :

MAIN TRUNK : MMM

- Meningeal

- Nerve to Medial Pterygoid

ANTERIOR DIVISION : Deep LAMBS

- Deep Temporal

- Lateral Pterygoid

- Masseteric

- Buccal - Sensory - Skin Of Cheek

POSTERIOR DIVISION : ALI

- Auriculotemporal : **ASAS**

- Auricular

- Superficial Temporal

- Articular to TMJ

- Secretomotor to Parotid Gland

- Lingual

- Inferior Alveolar : **IMA**

- Mylohyoid

- Anterior Belly of Digastric

FACIAL NERVE

FACIAL NERVE : NUCLEI : 4 NUCLEI SITUATED IN LOWER PONS : BSNL

- Branchiomotor / Motor Nucleus

- Superior Salivatoty Nucleus

- Nucleus of Tractus Solitarius

- Lacrimatory Nucleus

FACIAL NERVE : BRANCHES

WITHIN FACIAL CANAL : FG PSC

- Geater Petrosal Nerve

- Stapedius Nerve

- Chorda tympani

EXIT FROM STYLOMASTOID FORAMEN : PADS

- Posterior Auricular

- Digastric

- Stylohyoid

TERMINAL BRANCHES WITHIN PAROTID GLAND : Te Zy Bu Ma C

- Temporal

- Zygomatic

- Buccal

- Marginal Mandibular

- Cervical

COMMUNICATING BRANCHES WITH ADJACENT CRANIAL AND SPINAL NERVES

FACIAL NERVE : GANGLIA ASSOCIATED : GPS

- Geniculate Ganglion : Sensory

- Submandibular Ganglion : Parasympathetic

- Pterygopalatine Ganglion : Parasympathetic

CEREBELLUM

MORPHOLOGICAL AND FUNCTIONAL DIVISIONS : ARPAN

- **AR**chicerebellum
- **PA**leocerebellum
- **N**eocerebellum

FUNCTIONALITY : LONGITUDINAL ZONES : LIVE

- **L**ateral zone
- **I**ntermediate zone
- **VE**rmis

INFERIOR CEREBELLAR PEDUNCLE : AFFERENT TRACTS : VAST CORP

- **V**estibulocerebellar
- **A**nterior external arcuate fibres
- **S**triae medullaris
- **T**rigeminocerebellar
- **C**uneocerebellar (posterior external arcuate fibres)
- **O**livocerebellar
- **R**eticulocerebellar
- **P**osterior Spinocerebellar
- **P**arolivocerebellar

CEREBELLAR NUCLEI : LATERAL TO MEDIAL: Don't Eat Greasy Food

- Dentate - Neocerebellum
- Emboliform
- Globose
- [F]astigii with [F]locculonodular lobe - Archicerebellum

PALEOCEREBELLUM : NUCLEI : PEG

- Emboliform
- Globose

NEURONS : TYPES : GPS Basket

- EXCITATORY
- Granular Cells
- Inhibitory
- Golgi Cells
- Purkinje Cells
- Stellate Cells
- Basket Cells

BLOOD SUPPLY : SAP / SAB PV

- Superior cerebellar branch of Basilar artery
- Anterior inferior cerebellar branch of Basilar artery
- Posterior inferior cerebellar branch of Vertebral artery

FUNCTIONS : VC TRIMS

- Voluntary movements coordinate
- Comparator
- Tone, posture and equilibrium control
- Relay centre of all sensory information
- Ipsilateral influence
- Maintenance of muscle tone and posture
- Skilled movements – help planning and production along with cerebrum

CEREBELLAR COGNITIVE AFFECTIVE SYNDROME : CHARACTERISED BY : IAM NYSA

- Intention Tremors
- Adiadochokinesia
- Muscular Hypotonia
- Nystagmus
- Scanning Speech
- Ataxic or Unsteady Gait

CEREBRUM

CEREBRAL HEMISPHERE :

SURFACES : SUMI

- SUperolateral surface
- Medial surface
- Inferior surface : **IOT** (Intra Occular Tension)
- Orbital surface
- Tentorial surface

POLES : Front OT

- Frontal pole
- Occiptital pole
- Temporal pole

LOBES : CLAPP

- Central Sulcus
- Lateral Sulcus
- Parieto – Occipital Sulcus
- Preoccipital Notch

SULCI : TYPES : OLA

- Operculated Sulcus
- Limiting Sulcus
- Axial Sulcus

GYRI : PRE CENTRAL VS POST CENTRAL : SS

- Precentral : Motor
- Postcentral : Sensory

[M]EDIAL SURFACE : SULCI : [M]y CAPS

- CAllosal
- CAalcarine
- CIngulate
- Anterior Parolfactory
- Posterior Parolfactory
- Parieto - Occipital
- Suprasplenial Or Subparietal

FRONTAL LOBE : AREAS : MFP / BMP

- Motor Area
- Motor Speech Area Of Broca's
- Frontal Eyefield
- Premotor Area
- Prefrontal Area

FUNCTIONS OF CEREBRAL CORTEX : CAD

- Cerebral Dominance

- Contralateral Control of Voluntary Movements

- Associative Functions

- Discriminatory Aspects

DIENCEPHALON

DORSAL ASPECT : META THALAMUS

- METAthalamus

- Epithalamus

- Thalamus (Dorsal Thalamus)

VENTRAL ASPECT : VHS

- Hypothalamus

- Subthalamus (ventral thalamus)

GENICULATE BODIES : SLIM

- Superior Colliculi : [L]ateral Geniculate Body : [L]ight

- Inferior Colliculi : [M]edial Geniculate Body : [M]usic

HYPOTHALAMUS : PARTS : HOT MAMILLARY

- Optic Part

- Tuberal Part

- Mamillary Part

FUNCTIONS OF HYPOTHALAMUS : NEW BEEF GST

- Neurosecretion
- Biological Clocks
- Endocrine Control
- Emotion, Fear, Rage, Aversion, Pleasure And Reward
- Food And Water Intake Regulation
- General Autonomic Effect
- Sexual Behavior And Reproduction
- Temperature Regulation

CORPUS STRIATUM : CCL

- Caudate Nucleus
- Lentiform Nucleus

BLOOD SUPPLY OF SPINAL CORD AND BRAIN

ARTERIES OF BRAIN : VIN

- Vertebral Arteries
- Internal Carotid Arteries

VERTEBRAL ARTERIES : INTRACRANIAL BRANCHES : MAP

- Medullary Branches
- Meningeal Branches
- Anterior Spinal Artery

- Posterior Spinal Artery

- Posterior Inferior Cerebellar Artery

BASILAR ARTERY : BRANCHES : PALS

- Pontine Branches

- Posterior Cerebral Artery

- Anterior Inferior Cerebellar Artery

- Labyrinthine Artery

- Superior Cerebellar Artery

INTERNAL CAROTID ARTERY : BRANCHES : MAAP

- Middle Cerebral Artery

- Anterior Choroidal Artery

- Anterior Cerebral Artey

- Posterior Communicating Artery

CEREBRAL ARTERIES : I AM

- Internal Carotid Artery : Anterior Cerebral Middle Cerebral

- Basilar Artery : Posterior Cerebral

EMBRYOLOGY

MITOSIS : STEPS : IP MAT

- Interphase
- Prophase
- Metaphase
- Anaphase
- Telophase

MEIOSIS : PROPHASE : STAGES : LEZY PhD

- LEptotene
- ZYgotene
- Pachytene
- Diplotene

SPERMATOZOA : PARTS : His NaMe is PRINCe

- Head
- Neck
- Middle piece
- Principal piece

NECK : FBS CENTRIOLE

- Funnel shaped
- Basal body
- Spherical
- Centriole

CHROMOSOMAL ABNORMALITIES : TRADE IN

- TRAnslocation
- DEletion
- Duplication
- INversion

STROMA : LAYER : BSC

- Stratum Basale
- Stratum Spongiosum
- Stratum Compactum

HORMONES INFLUENCING OVULATION AND MENSTRUATION : FLOP

- FSH
- LH
- Oestrogens
- Progesterone

UMBILICAL CORD : CONTENTS : VIT WEB

- VITello – intestinal duct and remnants of the yolk sac
- Wharton's jelly
- Extra embryonic coelom (a small part)
- Blood vessels that pass from the embryo to placenta

IMPLANTATION : TYPES : ICE

- Interstitial Implantation
- Central Implantation
- Eccentric Implantation

DECIDUA : CAP

- Basalis
- CApsularis
- Pareitalis

ANCHORING VILLI : PARTS : TRAC

- TRuncus Chorii
- RAmi Chorii
- RAmuli Chorii

PHARYNGEAL ARCHES IST OR MANDIBULAR ARCH :

SKELETAL COMPONENTS : MMM IAS

- Malleus
- Most of the Mandible (Intramembraneous ossification)

- Incus
- Anterior Ligament of MALLEUS
- Sphenomandibular Ligament

MUSCLES : MM MATT

- Muscles of Mastication
- Mylohyoid
- Anterior Belly of Digastric
- Tensor Veli Palatini
- Levator Veli Palatini

SECOND PHARYNGEAL ARCH :
HYOID ARCH : SKELETAL ELEMENTS : SSSSS

- Stapes
- Styloid Process
- Stylohyoid Ligament
- Smaller (Lesser) Cornua of Hyoid
- Superior Half of body of Hyoid

MUSCLES : MO APPS

- Muscles of Facial expression
- Occipitofrontalis
- Auricular Muscles
- Platysma
- Posterior belly of Digastric
- Stylohyoid

POUCHES : DERIVATIVES

FIRST POUCH : PMT / PRE MEDICAL TEST

- [PHA]ryngo tympanic tube - PHA - FIRST

- Middle ear cavity

- Tympanic [A]ntrum - A - FIRST ALPHABET

SECOND POUCH : TT O AND U VOWELS

- T[O]nsil

- T[U]botymanic rece[SS] - S - SECOND

[THI]RD POUCH : THI

- THYmus

- Inferior Parathyroid Glands

PLACENTAL MEMBRANE / BARRIER : CONSTITUENTS : ES MS CS

- Endothelium of fetal blood vessels and its basement membrane

- Surrounding Mesoderm (connective tissue)

- Cytotrophoblast , and its basement membrane

- Syncytiotrophoblast

FUNCTIONS OF PLACENTA : My BEST

- Maternal antibodies (IgG gamma globulins) through placenta to fetus give immunity against some infections

- Barrier and prevents many bacteria and other harmful substances from reaching the fetus

- Excretion of carbon dioxide , urea , and other waste products by fetus

- Exchange of several substances between maternal and fetal blood

- Synthesises several hormones (syncytiotrophoblast)

- Transport of oxygen , water , electrolytes and nutrition from maternal to fetal blood

IMPLANTATION OUTSIDE THE UTERUS : IOT

- Interstitial Tubal Implantation

- Ovary

- Tubal Pregnancy

ANOMALIES OF PLACENTA : CFL BDS

- Circumvallate Placenta

- Fenestrated Placenta

- Lobed

- Bidiscoidal

- Diffuse

- Succenturiata

VARIATIONS IN ATTACHMENT OF UMBILICAL CORD TO PLACENTA : VIM
Furcate

- Vilamentous Insertion

- Marginal - Battledore Placenta

- Furcate

AMNIOTIC FLUID : FUNCTIONS : PAPA

- Provides Support For Delicate Tissues Of Growing Embryo Or Fetus

- Allows Free Movement

- Protects Fetus From External Injury

- Avoids Adhesion Of Fetus To Amnion

CELLS OF BONE : BOOST

- OSTeocytes

- OSTeoblasts

- OSTeoclasts

GROWTH OF A LONG BONE : ZONES : REP CAL

- Resting Cartilage

- Proliferating Cartilage

- Calcification

ANOMALIES OF BONE FORMATION : FOOD COMA

- Fibrous Dysplasia

- Osteogenesis Imperfecta

- Osteopetrosis

- Dyschondroplasia Or Enchondromatosis

- Cleido – Cranial Dysostosis

- Chondro – Osteo – Dystrophy

- Multiple Exostosis Or Diaphyseal Aclasis

- Achondroplasia

SOMITE : PARTS : SMD VIL

- Sclerotome   Ventromedial Part

- Myotome   Intermediate Part

- Dermatome   Lateral Part

PHYSIOLOGY MNEMONICS

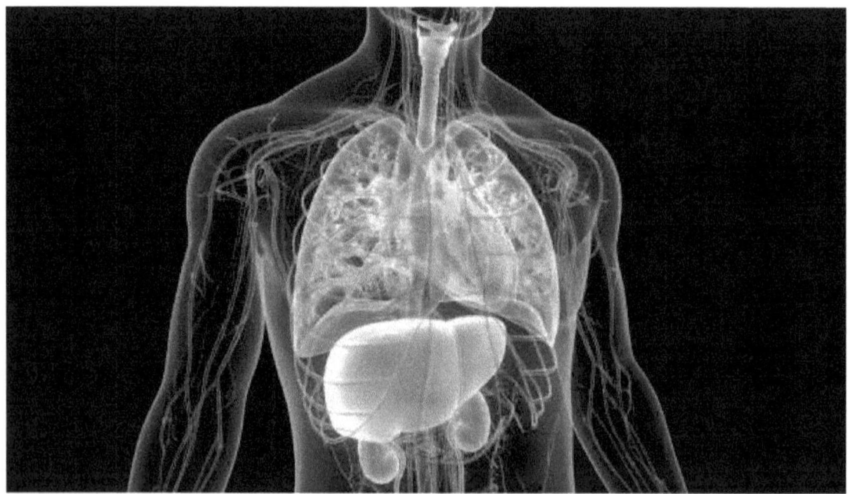

GENERAL INFORMATION

SKIN VASOCONSTRICTION AND TEMPERATURE

- CONServe heat - CONStriction of blood vessels

- COld skin - COnstriction of blood vessels

VITAMIN D : D → D

- Dermis (made in)

FLUID COMPARTMENTS : VOLUMES 12345

- 12 litres of interstitial fluid

- 3 litres plasma volume and 30 litres inside cells

- 45 litres total body water

POTASSIUM : PASSES OUTSIDE THE CELL (CAUSES) : PASSES

- Acidosis

- Starvation

- Stress

- Excercise

- Sodium chloride loss

ELECTRICAL CONDUCTIVITY OF TISSUES : LEAST TO MOST CONDUCTIVE : Be Careful To Shock My Best Nerve

- Bones

- Cartilage

- Tendon

- Skin

- Muscle

- Blood

- Nerve

COMPLIANCE OF LUNGS : FACTORS : COMPLIANCE

- Collagen Deposition (Fibrosis)

- Ossification Of Costal Cartilages

- Major Obesity

- Pulmonary Venous Congestion

- Lung Size

- Increased Expanding Pressure

- Age

- No Surfactant

- Chest Wall Scaring

- Emphysema

- All But L/A/E Decrease Compliance

BLOOD
ERYTHROPOIESIS

ERYTHROPOIESIS : SITE : IHM

- Intravascular - Between 3rd week to 3rd month of IUL
- Hepatic - Between 3rd month to 5th month of IUL
- Myeloid - In Red Bone Marrow - 5th month ownwards

ERYTHROPOIESIS STAGES : PBPO RE
(BPO – Bank Probationary Officer) / PEIL RE

- Proerythroblast (Pronormoblast)
- Basophilic Erythroblast (Early Normoblast)
- Polychromatic Erythroblast (Intermediate Normoblast)
- Orthochromatophilic Erythroblast (Late Normoblast)
- Reticulocyte
- Erythrocyte

HAEMATOPOIETIC GROWTH FACTORS : SET
GIC / GIC SET

- Stem Cell Factor (SCF)
- Erythropoietin (EPO)
- Thrombopoietin
- Granulocyte - macrophage colony stimulating factor (GM -CSF)
- Interleukins (ILs)
- Colony Stimulating Factor (CSF – 1) / MCF

FATE OF HAEMOGLOBIN

- URobilinogen - URine

- STercobilinogen - Stool

HAEMOGLOBIN ABNORMALITIES : HEREDITARY : HTP

- Haemoglobinopathies - Eg : Sickle Cell Anemia

- Thalassemias - Alpha and Beta

- Porphyrias (Excess activity of ALA synthase enzyme)

MACROCYTIC ANEMIA : CAUSES : ABCDEF

- Alcohol + liver disease

- B12 deficiency

- Compensatory reticulocytosis (blood loss and haemolysis)

- Drug (cytotoxic and AZT) / Dysplasia (Marrow problems)

- Endocrine (hypothyroidism)

- Folate deficiency / Fetus (Pregnancy)

POLYCYTHEMIA : TYPES : P – P

- Primary - Polycythemia vera

- Secondary

WHITE BLOOD CELL RELATIVE CONCENTRATIONS : Never Let Monkeys Eat Bananas

From Greatest To Least

- Neutrophils (65%)

- Lymphocytes (25%)

- Monocytes (6%)

- Eosinophils (3%)

- Basophils (1%)

LEUKOCYTES : GRANULATED AND AGRANULATED

- BEN Loves Money

- Basophils, Eosinophils, Neutrophils - Granulocytes

- Lymphocytes, Monocytes - Agranulocytes

IMMUNE MECHANISM : COMPONENTS : CC

Cellular components : MLD

- Monocytes

- Lymphocytes

- Langerhans Cells

- Dendritic Cells

Chemical components : IC

- Immunoglobulins

- Cytokines

LYMPHOCYTES : CLASSES : NAME TB

- Natural Killer Cells (NK Cells)

- Memory Cells

- T lymphocytes

- B lymphocytes

FUNCTIONS OF MACROPHAGES : LAKHS

- Lymphocyte Mediated Immunity (Help in)

- Acute Inflammation (Assist to remove antigen in)

- Kupffer's cells remove bacteria of portal venous blood.

- Haematopoietic Factors (Secrete some)

- Scavengers by removing dead RBCs, foreign bodies (Act as).

PLATELETS

PLATELETS : IDAS / SADI

- Inactive - Disc like

- Active - Spherical

PLATELETS : STRUCTURES WITHIN CYTOSOL: GMCT [Government Medical College Thiruvananthapuram]

- Granules

- Golgi Apparatus

- Mitochondria

- Contractile Elements

- Tubules

PLATELETS : GRANULES

AL[PHA] GRANULES : CONTAIN : [FA]CTORS

- Fibronectin

- Factor V

- Factor VII

- PF4 (Platelet Factor 4)

- PDGF (Platelet Derived Growth Factor)

- VMF

- Also produce TGF Beta

DENSE GRANULES : CONTAIN : CASH

- Calcium (Ca++)

- ADP

- ATP

- Serotonin (5HT)

- Histamine

ANTI[GEN] : [GEN]

- AGGLUTINO[GEN]

- ANTIBODY : AGGLUTININ

BLOOD COAGULATION

CLOTTING FACTORS : STARTING AND ENDING WITH FIBRIN

- I : FIBRIN

- XIII : FIBRIN STABILISING FACTOR

CLOTTING FACTORS : II - PT III - TP

- II : PROTHROMBIN

- III : THROMBOPLASTIN

CLOTTING FACTORS : V, VII - [VEN]

- V : PROACCELERIN

- VII : PROCO[NVE]RTIN : SE[VEN]

CIRCULATORY ANTICOAGULANTS : [HEPA IN]

- HEPAr[in]

- Prote[in] C and Prote[in] S

- Antithromb[in]

VON WILLEBRAND FACTOR (vWF) : SYNTHESIS AND FUNCTION : vMF

- Vascular Endothelium

- Megakaryocytes

- Factor VIII Carrier

BLEEDING TIME : SINGLE WORD

- Duke's method
- Ivy's method

CLOTTING TIME : TWO WORDS

- Wright's capillary tube method
- Lee and White's method

INTRINSIC VERSUS EXTRINSIC PATHWAY TESTS

- PTT : Play Table Tennis : Inside : Intrinsic pathway
- PT : Play Tennis : Outside : Extrinsic pathway

COMMON LABORATORY TESTS FOR BLEEDING DISORDERS : ABC PT

- Activated Partial Thromboplastin Time
- Bleeding Time
- Clotting Time
- Clot Retraction Time
- Prothrombin Time
- Platelet Counting

PURPURA : BP CAP NORMAL

- BT Prolonged
- CT
- APTT and PT are NORMAL

PLASMA PROTEINS

PLASMA PROTEINS : GALF

- Globulin

- ALbumin

- Fibrinogen

ALPHA ONE PLASMA PROTEINS : ATAFEL

- Alpha 1 Anti Trypsin

- Alpha 1 Acid glycoprotein

- Alpha 1 FEtoprotein

- Alpha 1 Lipoproteins (HDL)

ALPHA TWO PLASMA PROTEINS : MANCH

- Alpha 2 MAcroglobulin

- Alpha 2 ANtiplasmin

- Alpha 2 Ceruloplasmin

- Alpha 2 Haptoglobin

BETA GLOBULINS : BPTH

- Beta lipoproteins(LDL)

- Plasminogen

- Trasferrin

- Hemopexin

PLASMA PROTEINS : FUNCTIONS : O BAP

- Oncotic Pressure

- Buffer

- Antibody carrier – in their gamma globulin fraction

- Procoagulant Proteins

- Physiologic substance and drugs carrier - hormones , bilirubin and so on

INTRINSIC NERVE SUPPLY OF GIT : IAM

- Auerbach's Plexus and

- Meissner's Plexus

DIGESTIVE SYSTEM

SALIVARY GLAND

SALIVON: SECRETORY UNIT OF SALIVARY GLAND : SAI S

- Acinus

- Intercalated Duct

- Striated Duct

SALIVARY SECRETIONS : VARIETIES : SSS

- Spontaneous

- Stimulated

SALIVA : COMPOSITION : ORGANIC : MAP GELL

- Mucus

- Alpha amylase OR

- Ptyalin

- Glycoprotein

- EDGF

- Lysozyme

- Lingual Lipase

STOMACH

GASTRIC JUICE : ORGANIC : HB

- HCL

- Bicarbonates

INORGANIC : EMI

- Enzymes

- Mucus

- Intrinsic Factor

INHIBITION OF HCL SECRETION : EH GAS

- Enterogastrone

- Hyperosmotic Gastric Chime

- GIP

- Acid Chyme

- Somatostatin

- Secretin

FUNDIC GLANDS : CELLS : PNS

- Peptic Cells / Chief Cells

- Parietal Cells / Oxyntic Cells

- Neck Mucous Cells

- Stem Cells

PANCREAS

PANCREATIC JUICE : ENZYMES : PROTEASES : PCT

- Proelastase

- Procarboxypeptidase A

- Procarboxypeptidase B

- Chymotrypsin

- Trypsin

ENDOPEPTIDASES : [PSIN]

- Pe[PSIN]

- Try[PSIN]

- Chymotry[PSIN]

- Elastase

E[XO]PEPTIDASES : [OX]

- Carb[OX]ypeptidases

FUNCTIONS OF BILE : DCC IMA

- Digestion and absorption of fat

- Choleretic action of bile salts

- Cholesterol kept in solution in bile by bile salts

- Cathartic / Purgative (mild) action - bile salts

- Inhibit endogenous synthesis of cholesterol by liver

- Antibacterial Action

BILE : CONTROL OF SECRETION : BAGS

- Bile Acids

- Gastrin

- Secretin

FUNCTIONS OF LIVER : BILD HOMES

- BILe Secretion

- Detoxicating Functions

- Hormone Inactivation

- Metabolic Functions

- Synthetic Functions

- Storage Function

SITES OF ABSORPTION:
DUODENUM : DIC

- Iron

- Calcium

ILEUM : BB

- B12

- Bile Salt

GI : SECRETION BY CELLS

- G CELLS - GASTRIN   G - G

- S CELLS - SECRETIN   S - S

- PARIETAL CELLS - HCL   PH

GI : SECRETION BY CELLS : ICDS

- I CELLS - CHOLECYSTOKININ

- D CELLS - SOMATOSTATIN

[PARI]ETAL CELLS : PRODUCE : [PARI]

- Produce Acid (HCL) and

- Release Intrinsic Factor

RESPIRATORY SYSTEM

MUSCLES OF INSPIRATION : DE SC ST

- Diaphragm
- External Intercostals Muscles

ACCESSORY MUSCLES OF INSPIRATION : SC ST

- Scalene Muscles
- STernocleidomastoids

MUSCLES OF EXPIRATION : TREIN

- Transverse Abdominis
- Rectus Abdominis
- External Oblique
- Internal Oblique
- Internal Intercostals

WORK DONE IN BREATHING : RESISTANCES : EAT

- Elasticity
- Airway Resistance
- Tissue Resistance

RESPIRATORY CENTRE : DESCRIPTION : MRP UP AC LOW

- Medullary Respiratory Centre

- Pneumotaxic Centre - UPper Part of Pons

- Apneustic Centre - LOWer part of pons

MEDULLARY RESPIRATORY CENTRE : PARTS : VEDI

- Ventral Group of Respiratory Neuron   Expirtion

- Dorsal Group of Respiratory Neuron   Inspiration

RESISTANCE AGAINST PASSAGE OF GASES : ACRI RR

- Alveolocapillary Membrane

- Capillary Plasma

- RBC membrane plus ICF in RBC

- Reaction Rate

HYPOXIA : TYPES : HASH

- Hypoxic Hypoxia

- Anaemic Hypoxia

- Stagnant Hypoxia

- Histotoxic Hypoxia

PERIODIC BREATHING : BC

- Biot's Breathing

- Cheyne - Stokes Breathing

LUNGS

LUNG RECEPTORS : HiJ

- Hering - Breuer reflex
- Juxtacapillary / J receptors

LUNG DEFENCE MECHANISM : PM CML

- Physical - Physiological Mechanism
- MucoCiliary Defence Mechanism
- Macrophage
- Lung fluids

OCCUPATIONAL EXPOSURES : BSP

- Byssinosis
- Silicosis
- Pneumoconiosis of the coal miners

CIGARETTE SMOKING : CAUSES : CCC

- Cancer - Lung Cancer
- CHD (Coronary Heart Diseases)
- COPD

CARCINOGENS IN CIGARETTE : HY TARPOLYN

- HYdralazine

- TAR

- POLY - Nuclear Hydrocarbons

- Nitrosamines

LUNG FUNCTION TESTS
LUNG VOLUMES : TIER

- Tidal Volume

- ERV (Expiratory Reserve Volume)

- RV (Residual Volume)

LUNG CAPACITIES : FUVIN

- Functional Residual Capacity

- Vital Capacity

- INspiratory Capacity

NON RESPIRATORY FUNCTIONS OF LUNGS : LMNO

- Lung Defence Mechanism

[ME]tabolic [E]ndocrine functions : [ME] BAD

- Biosynthetic - Eicosanoids

- Activation/Biotransformaion - Angiotensin I to Angiotensin II by ACE

- Degradation / Removal - Bradykinin, PGE2, PGE1, LTs

- Non Respiratory Functions

Others : WATER

- WATER   Balance

- Acid Base Balance

- Thermoregulation

CARDIOVASCULAR SYSTEM
HEART

ELECTROPHYSIOLOGIC PROPERTIES OF HEART MUSCLES : ACE

- Autorhythmicity
- Conductivity
- Excitability

HEART : CONDUCTION PATHWAY : SAB RLP

- SA Node
- AV Node
- Bundle of His
- Right and Left Bundles
- Purkinje Fibres

CARDIAC CYCLE : ICR RPD IRV R DAS

- Isovolumetric Contraction
- Rapid Ejection Phase
- Reduced Ejection Phase
- ProtoDiastolic Phase of Ventricles
- Isovolumetric Relaxation of Ventricles
- Rapid Filling Phase of Ventricles
- Diastasis
- Atrial Systole

CARDIAC OUTPUT : MEASUREMENT : CDT

- Cardiac Catheterization - Fick Principle

- Dye Method

- Thermal Dilution Method

CARDIAC OUTPUT : ALTERATIONS : PPP

PHYSIOLOGICAL : SPERM

- Sleep

- Posture

- Excitement

- Rage and Panic

- Muscular Excercise

PATHOLOGICAL : MASTH

- Myocardial Infarction

- Acidosis

- Septicaemia

- Thyrotoxicosis

- Haemorrhage

PHARMACOLOGICAL (DRUG INDUCED) : BCD

- Beta Adrenergic Blockers

- Beta Adrenergic Stimulants (Specific)

- Calcium Channel Blockers

- Caffiene

- Dobutamine

- Digitalis

VENOUS RETURNS : FACTORS INFLUENCING : CV MGR

- Cardiac Output

- Venomotor Tone

- Muscle Pump

- Gravity

- Respiratory Pump

MEAN ARTERIAL PRESSURE : DTP

- MAP = Diastolic BP + 1/3 Pulse Pressure

BLOOD PRESSURE : FACTORS AFFECTING : SAME C

- Sex

- Sleep

- Age

- Meals

- Muscular Excercise

- Emotion

- Exposure to Cold

- Circadian Rhythm

ECG : LEADS : FRONTAL PLANE LEADS : LEADS I II III : BEST

- Bipolar Leads
- Einthoven's Leads
- STandard Leads

HEART VALVES

- TRIcuspid on Right
- Bicuspid / MitraL on Left

[T]H[IN] FILAMENT : MADE UP OF : [TIN]

- Ac[TIN]
- [T]ropomyos[IN]
- [T]ropon[IN]

TROPONIN : SUBUNITS : ITC

- Troponin I
- Troponin T
- Troponin C

HEART VALVES : CLOSURE SEQUENCE :
Many Things are Possible

- Mitral
- Tricuspid
- Aortic
- Pulmonary

HEART : CONDUCTION PATHWAY : SAB Purkinje

- SA Node
- AV Node
- Bundle of His
- Purkinje Fibres

OSTEOCLAST : Builds Bone

- Consumes Bone

HEART VALVES : SEQUENCE OF CLOSURE : MI TRAP / MITRA P

- Tricuspid
- Aortic
- Pulmonic

MEAN ARTERIAL PRESSURE : DP POT PP

- Diastolic Pressure Plus One Third of Pulse Pressure

BP DECREASING HORMONES : HAA VIP BP

- Histamine
- Acetyicholine
- Atrial Natriuretic Peptide (ANP)
- Vasoactive Intestinal Polypeptide (VIP)
- Bradykinin
- Prostaglandin

BLOOD VESSELS : HOMONAL CONTROL : A RED

- Adrenaline

- ADH

- ANP

- Renin - angiotensin

- Endothelin

- Dopamine

KOROTKOV SOUNDS : TAPS MURA GO MUD

- Phase I   Tap sound   SBP
- Phase II   MUR   Auscultatory gap
- Phase III GOnging
- Phase IV   MUffled
- Phase V   Disappear   DBP

LYMPH : FUNCTIONS : FILL

- Fluid recovery

- Immunity

- Lipid Absorption

LYMPH : COMPOSTION : ECLIPSe

- Electrolytes

- Cells

- LIPids

- Protein S

ENDOCRINOLOGY

CHEMICAL SIGNALS : CG PAN / CN GAP / CNG AP

- Classical Hormones
- Gastro Intestinal Hormones
- Paracrine Hormones
- Autacoids Or Local Hormones
- Autocrines
- Neurotransmitters

HORMONES AND OTHER CHEMICALS : PASTE

- Proteins or Peptides
- Aminoacid Derivatives
- STeroids
- Eicosanoids

RECEPTORS : Multi National Company

- Membrane bound
- Nuclear or
- Cytoplasmic

MEMBRANE BOUND : GNM

- G Protein Coupled
- No G Protein Required

SECOND MESSENGERS : CID

- CAMP

- Ca++

- IP3

- DAG

CONTROL OF HORMONE SECRETION : HAF CNS

- Hypothalamic Control

- Anterior Pituitary

- Feed Back

- Circadian Rhythm

- Neural

- Stress

FUNCTIONS OF HORMONES : HCG REPRODUCTION

- Homeostasis

- Combating Emergency

- Growth

- Reproduction

PITUITARY HORMONES : FLAG TOP / GOAT FLAP

- Follicle Stimulating Hormone
- Lutinizing Hormone
- Adrenocorticotropin Hormone
- Growth Hormone
- Thyroid Stimulating Hormone
- Oxytocin
- Prolactin

THYROID HORMONES : TTT / TTC

- T4
- T3
- ThyroCalcitonin

THYROXINE : BIOSYNTHESIS : IOC (Indian Oil Corporation)

- Iodide Trapping
- Oxidation of Iodide
- Organification
- Coupling

FUNCTIONS OF CALCIUM WITHIN THE CELL :

RELEASE OF SECOND MESSENGER CAUSES VASCULAR SPASM IN PHASE TWO MUSCULAR CONTRACTION

- Release of

- Second Messenger

- Vascular Spasm

- In Phase Two

- Muscular Contraction

CALCIUM BINDING PROTEINS WITHIN THE CELLS : CT

- Calmodulin

- Calbindin

- Troponin

FUNCTIONS OF PARATHORMONE : CORE

- Conversion of vit D into calcitriol (facilitates)

- Calcium absorption facilitates in jejunum

- Osteoblastic activity intensified - increases bone resorption

- REnal tubules - increase calcium reabsorption , phosphate excretion

FUNCTIONS OF VITAMIN D (CALCITRIOL) : BONE GK

- Bone
- GIT
- Kidney

FUNCTIONS OF SUPRARENAL CORTICAL HORMONES : 3P'S

- Physiological Actions
- Pharmacological Actions
- Permissive Actions

NERS : PARTICIPATING HORMONES : CAT

- Cortisol
- ACTH
- ADH
- Adrenaline
- Thyroid hormones

TARGET CELLS OF ALDOSTERONE : SWEAT BRAIN GK

- SWEAT glands
- Brain
- GIT
- Kidney

CLASSIFICATION OF HORMONES PRODUCED BY ANTERIOR PITUITARY AND PLACENTA : GPS

- Glycoprotein Hormones
- Pomc Derivatives
- Somatotropic and Related Hormone   Family

EFFECTS OF INSULIN ON TARGET CELLS : ELISA

- LIver
- Skelatal Muscles
- Adipocytes

CONTROL OF INSULIN SECRETION : SHONE

- Substrate Control
- Hormonal Control
- Neural Control

GROWTH PROMOTING FACTORS : PINE

- PDGF
- IGF - 1
- NGF
- EGF

AUTACOIDS : CLASSIFICATION : LAP

- Lipid Autacoids

- Amine Autacoids

- Peptide Autacoids

[PROGESTE]RONE : ACTIONS : [PROGESTE]

- Produce Cervical Mucous

- Relax Uterine Smooth Muscle

- Oxytocin Sensitivity Down

- Gonadotropin (FSH/LH) Secretions Down

- Endometrial Spiral Arteries and secretions up

- Sustain Pregnancy

- Temperature Up / Tit development

- Excitability of myometrium down

OESTROGEN : FUNCTIONS : OESTROGEN

- Organ (Sex) development

- Endocrine : FSH and LH regulation

- Secondary sex characteristics development / Sex drive increase

- Tropic for pregnancy

- Receptor synthesis (of progesterone,oestrogen ,LH)

- Osteoporosis decrease (inhibits bone resorption)

- Granulosa cell development

- Endocrine : increases prolactin secretion , but then blocks its effect

- Nipple development

PROLACTIN : [PRO]

- [PRO]duce milk

[O]xytocin : [O]

- [O]oze milk (release)

GUT INTRINSIC INNERVATION : (M→M) (S→S)

- Myentric : Motility

- Submucosal : Secretion and blood flow

HYPERTHYROIDISM : SIGNS AND SYMPTOMS : THYROIDISM

- Tremor

- Heart rate up

- Yawning (fatigability)

- Restlessness

- Oligomenorrhea and amenorrhea

- Intolerance to heat

- Diarrhoea

- Irritability

- Sweating

- Muscle wasting and wait loss

ADRENAL CORTEX LAYERS AND PRODUCTS

GFR GLOMERULAR FILTRATION RATE : MGA / ACS

- Granulosa : Mineralocorticoid (Aldosterone)

- Fasciculata : Glucorticoid (Cortisol)

- Reticularis : Androgens (Sex steroids)

ADRENAL GLAND : FUNCTIONS : ACTH

- Adrenergic functions

- Catabolism of proteins / Carbohydrate metabolism

- T cell immunomodulation

- Hyper / Hypotension (blood pressure control)

SERTOLI CELL : IAM B RENT

- Inhibin

- Activin

- Mullerian regression factor

- Blood Testis Barrier

- Receptors for FSH and Testosterone

- Estradiol from Testosterone

- Nutrition to germ cells

- Testosterone converted to 5 alpha DHT

PROSTRATIC SECRETION : ECF

- Enzymes
- Citrate
- Fructose

FRUCTOSE AND CITRATE : FFF

- Fuels for spermatozoa in
- Female genital tract

SEMINAL PLASMA : CAP FFA / CAP Free Fatty Acids

- Citric acid
- Ascorbic acid
- Prostaglandins
- Fructose
- Fibrinogen as well as fibrinolytic mechanism
- Acid phosphatase

TESTIS : HORMONES PRODUCED : AEI (VOWELS)

- Androgens
- Activin
- Estrogen
- Inhibin

ANDROGENS : DATE

- DHEA
- DHT
- Androstenedione
- TEstosterone

ANDROGENS : PRODUCED BY : TELS / ATLES / ATLEZ

- Testis
- LEydig cells of testis
- Zona reticularis of supra renal cortex

STEROIDOGENIC TISSUE : O ATP

- Ovary
- Adrenal cortex
- Testis
- Placenta

ANTRAL FLUID : COMPOSITION : FLUid PEP MP

- FSH
- LH
- Prolactin
- Estrogen
- Progesterone

- Mucopolysaccharide

- Plasminogen

MENSTRUAL CYCLE : FOLLICULAR BLEEDING

- Follicular / Proliferative phase

- Ovulation phase

- Luteal / Secretory phase

- Bleeding phase

FEMALE SEX HORMONES : HOP

- Hypothalamic

- Ovarian

- Pituitary / Placental

RECEPTORS OF ESTROGEN : BHORe

- Breast

- Hypothalamus

- Osteoblasts

- Reproductive tracts

ACTIONS OF ESTROGEN : M BCD

- Metabolic actions

- Behavioural changes / Actions on brain

- Coagulability of blood

- Developmental action

METABOLISM
ENZYMES

ENZYME ACTIVITIES : FACTORS INFLUENCING : TIPS

- Temperature

- Ionic Effects

- PH

- Substrate Concentration

MAO ISOENZYMES : LOCATIONS : (A→A, B→B)

- MAO –A : Adrenergic Peripheral Structures

- : Alimentary Mucosa (Intestine)

- MAO – B : Brain

- : Blood Platelets

CAROTID [S]INU[S] : [SS]

- Measures pre[SS]ure

CAROTID B[O]DY : [O]

- Measures O2

PROTEIN C , PROTEIN S : FUNCTIONS : CS

- Clot Stoppers (Inhibit coagulation)

RENAL SYSTEM

URINARY TRACT : UUU / 3U

- Ureter

- Urinary Bladder

- Urethra

RENAL TUBULE : PARTS : BPL

- Bowman's Capsule

- Proximal Tubule

- Loop Of Henle

JUXTA GLOMERULAR APPARATUS : JUMALA

- JUxta Glomerular Cells

- Macula Densa

- Lacis Cells

REGULATION OF RENAL BLOOD FLOW : DAS

- Dopamine

- Angiotensin II

- Sympathetic Stimulation And Nor Adrenalin (NA)

AUTOREGULATION OF RENAL BLOOD FLOW : BHK

- Brain
- Heart
- Kidney

TUBULAR FUNCTIONS : COARSE / SARC

- Concentration and
- Acidification of tubular fluid
- Reabsorption
- Secretion

SECRETION BY PT : IPC DRUGS

- Iodinated dyes (some)
- PAH
- Creatinine
- Drugs like penicillin and salicylates

FUNCTIONS OF DISTAL SEGMENT : CRASE PCM DRUGS

- Concentration of urine
- Reabsorption (further) of $Na+$, $Cl-$, and water
- Acidification of urine
- Secretion of Potassium , Calcium ,Magnesium and
- DRUGS(some)

CLEARANCE TESTS : GIC PAR

- GFR

- Inulin Clearance

- Creatinine Clearance

- RBF - PAHA test

HORMONES PRODUCED BY KIDNEYS : HERO

- Erythropoietin

- Renin

- One twenty five dihydroxy cholecalciferol

HORMONES AFFECTING ON RENAL FUNCTIONS : PAN

- Parathormone

- Progesterone

- Aldosterone

- ADH

- ANP

MAJOR FUNCTIONS OF KIDNEY : WEAR

- Water and electrolyte balance

- Excretion of waste products

- Acid base balance - maintanance

- Regulatory hormone production (erythropoietin)

SKELETAL MUSCLES, SMOOTH MUSCLES

MUSCLE SARCOMERE : (A – A) (I - I)

- [A] Band : D[A]rk Band

- [I] Band : L[I]ght Band

MUSCLE SARCOMERE : HAZIB (B for Band)

- H line in A Band

- Z Disc in I Band

NERVOUS SYSTEM

CUTANEOUS RECEPTORS

TOUCH RECEPTORS : TMM

- Meissner's Corpuscles

- Merkel's Disc

PRESSURE RECEPTORS : P - P

- Pacinian Corpuscles

TEMPERATURE RECPTOR :

COLD : CK

- Krause's end Organ

W[AR]M : [AR] [RA]

- [RA]ffini's end Organ

NERVE FIBRES

SENSITIVITY TO HYPOXIA : MOST TO LEAST : HYBAC

- B>A>C

SENSITIVITY TO COCAINE AND LOCAL ANAESTHETICS : CCBA

- C>B>A

SENSITIVITY TO PRESSURE : PABC

- A>B>C

EXCITATORY NEUROTRANSMITTERS : HAANG

- Histamine

- Aspartate

- Acetylcholine

- Nitric Oxide

- Glutamate

INHIBITORY NEUROTRANSMITTERS : G GDS

- GABA

- Glycine

- Dopamine

- Serotonine

NEUROTRANSMITTERS IN SLEEP : SAND

- Serotonin (Initiates Sleep)

- Acetylcholine (Ach)

- Norepinephrine

- Dopamine (causes arousal from sleep ie, wakefullness)

PYRAMIDAL TRACTS : LAC

- Lateral and

- Anterior Corticospinal Tracts

LI[MB]IC SYSTEM : [MB]

- Major efferent from li[MB]ic system goes to : [M]id [B]rain reticular formation

- Main function of L[IMBIC] system : [EM]otional [BE]haviour [C]ontrol

AUDITORY PATHWAY : I MAST / IMA ST

- Inferior Colliculus

- Medial Geniculate Body

- Auditory Area Of Brain

- Superior Temporal Gyrus

ARGYLL - ROBERTSON PUPIL : ARP

- Accomodation Reflex Present

- Pupillary Reflex Absent

HYPOTHALAMUS : GENERAL FUNCTIONS : LATE

- Libido

- Appetite

- Temperature

- Emotion

CHEMORECEPTOR TRIGGER ZONE : DHS MO

- Dopamine

- Histamine

- Serotonin

- Muscarinic Opioids

BIOCHEMISTRY MNEMONICS

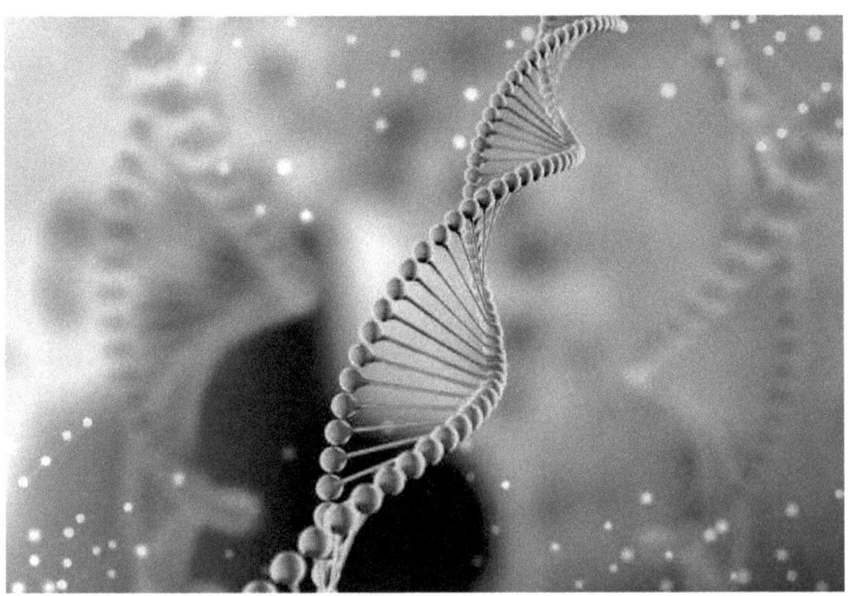

CARBOHYDRATES : CLASSIFICATION : MoDi OPol

- Monosaccharides
- Disaccharides
- Oligosaccharides
- Polysaccharides
- GLUCOSE : ALDOSE
- FRUC[TOSE] : [TOSE]
- KE[TOSE]

ISOMERISM : CLASSIFICATION : DEAP

- D and L Isomer
- Epimer
- Anomer (alpha and beta)
- Aldose and Ketose
- Pyranose and Furanose

IMPORTANT CHEMICAL REACTIONS OF MONOSACCHARIDES :

AEIO R

- Acetylation
- Acids
- Alkali
- Ester Formation

- Iodo Compounds

- Oxidation

- Osazone Formation

- Reduction

DISACCHARIDES : LMS College

- Lactose - Milk Sugar

- Maltose - Malt Sugar

- Sucrose - Crane Sugar

POLYSACCHARIDES : G ICDS

- Glycogen

- Inulin

- Cellulose

- Dextrin

- Starch

LIPIDS

MUCOSUBSTANCES : MMM / MGM

- Mucoproteins (Glycoproteins)

- Mucopolysaccharides (Heteropolysaccharides)

MUCOPOLYSACCHARIDES : MHC BHK

- Heteropolysaccharides

- Chondroitin Sulphates

- Blood group substances

- Heparin

- Keratosulphate

COMPOUND LIPIDS : LPGAS

- Lipoproteins

- Phospholipid

- Glycolipids

- Aminolipid

- Sulpholipid

PHOSPHOLIPIDS : PLP LPSC

- Phosphatidic Acid and Phosphatidyl Glycerols

- Lecithins (Phosphatidylcholine)

- Phosphatidyl Serine

- Phosphatidyl Inositol (Lipositol or Phosphoinositides)

- Lysophospholipids

- Plasmalogens

- Sphingomyelins

- Cephalins (Phosphatidyl Ethanolamine)

AMINOACIDS

ESSENTIAL AMINOACIDS : HILL AT TVPM

- Histidine Isoleucine Leucine Lycine Arginine

- Threonine Tryptophan Valine Phenyl Alanine Methionine

SEMI ESSENTIAL AMINOACIDS : SHA

- Histidine

- Arginine

BASIC AMINO ACIDS : HLA

- Histidine < Lysine < Arginine

AMINOACIDS WITH AROMATIC RING : AAAA

- All Aromatic Aminoacids derived from Alanine

AMINOACIDS WITH AROMATIC RING : HTTP

- Histidine

- Tryptophan

- Tyrosine

- Phenylalanine

PHOTOCHROMACITY ORDER : MAXIMUM TO MINIMUM : TTP

- Emits UV at wavelength 250 - 290 nm (esp at 280 nm)
- Tryptophan
- Tyrosine
- Phenylalanine

STRENGTH OF DIFFERENT BONDS : STRONGEST TO WEAKEST : CDE HV

- Covalent
- Disulphide
- Electrostatic / Ionic
- Hydrogen Bond
- Vanderwall Forces (Weakest)

MELATONIN VS MELANIN : [TO]

- Mela[TO]nin - Synthesized from Tryp[TO]phan
- Malanin - Synthesized from Tyrosine

GLUTAMATE IS PRECURSOR OF : GAP

- Glutamine
- Arginine
- Proline

HAEMOGLOBIN SYNTHESIS : AMINOACIDS REQUIRED : HLA

- Histidine

- Lysine

- Arginine

KERATIN : FORMED BY : HLA

- Histidine

- Lysine

- Arginine

P[URI]NE CATABOLISM : [URI]

- [URI]c acid

CELL DIVISION : P MAT

- Prophase

- Metaphase

- Anaphase

- Telophase

FASTING STAGE : FAS PHOS

- Phosphorylation Enzymes are active

BUFFERS IN BLOOD : BPH

- Bicarbonate Buffer

- Phosphate Buffer

- Protein Buffer

- Haemoglobin Buffer

TRANSPORT THROUGH BIOLOGICAL CELL MEMBRANE : PF ATP

- Passive Diffusion

- Facilitated Transfer

- Active Transport

- Transport of Ions

- Pinocytosis

DEDUCTION OF RADIOACTIVITY : GASSI / SAGI

- Geiger Counters

- Autoradiography

- Semi Conductor Detectors

- Scintillation

- Ionisation

- Ionisation Chambers

PHYSIOLOGICALLY ACTIVE PEPTIDES : GO BAC

- Glutathione

- Oxytocin and Vasopressin

- Bradykinin

- Angiotensin

- Antibiotics

- Carnosine

PROTEINS

SIMPLE PROTEINS : HP GAS

- Histones

- Prolamines

- Protamines

- Globulins

- Glutelins

- Albumins

- Scleroproteins

CONJUGATED PROTEINS : CFL P GNM

- Chromoproteins

- Flavoproteins

- Lipoproteins

- Phosphoproteins

- Glycoproteins

- Nucleoproteins

- Metalloproteins

DERIVED PROTEINS :
PRIMARY : PCM

- Proteans

- Coagulated Proteins

- Metaproteins

SECONDARY : PPP

- Proteoses

- Peptones

- Peptides

NUCLEOTIDES

PYR[I]M[I]D[I]NES : I RING STRUCTURES : CUT

- Cytosine

- Uracil

- Thymine

PURINE BASES : [NINE]

- Ade[NINE]

- Gua[NINE]

NUCLEOSIDES CONTAINING PURINE BASES : GAIN

- Guanosine

- Adenosine

- INosine

NATURALLY OCCURRING NUCLEOTIDES : SAVIT ICU

- S - Adenosylmethionine

- ATP and ADP

- VITamin Nucleotides

- Inosine Monophosphate

- Cyclic AMP

- Cyclic GMP

- Cytosine Derivatives

- Uridine Nucleotide Derivatives

SYNTHETIC   DERIVATIVES : CAT

- Cytarabine

- Allopurinol

- Azathioprine

- Aminophylline

- Theophylline

- 6 –Thioguanine and 6 - Mercaptopurine

NUCLEIC ACIDS AND CHROMATIN

CLASSES OF RNA : RMS

- rRNA

- mRNA

- sRNA (tRNA)

NUCLEOPROTEINS : PHD R

- Protamines

- Histones

- Deoxyribonucleoproteins

- Ribonucleoproteins

METALLOPORPHYRINS : HEM CT / C METH

- HEMoglobin

- Erythrocruorins

- Myoglobins

- Catalases

- Cytochromes

- Tryptophan Pyrrolase

ENZYMES

ENZYMES CLASSIFICATION : OTH LIL

- Oxidoreductases

- Transferases

- Hydrolases

- Ligases

- Isomerases

- Lyases

ENZYME SPECIFICITY : GROw Bag

- Group Specificity

- Reaction Specificity

- Optical Specificity

- Bond Specificity

FACTORS INFLUENCING ACTION OF ENZYMES : PO RTI ACt

- pH

- Oxidation

- Radiation

- Temperature

- Inhibiting Agents

- Anti Enzymes

- Contact between Enzyme and Substrate

- Concentration of Enzyme and Substrate

- Co enzymes and Activators

ENZYME KINETICS : COMPETITIVE VS NON - COMPETITIVE

	Km	V max
COMPETITIVE	Increases	No Change
NON - COMPETITIVE	No Change	Decreases

BASED ON CHEMICAL CHARACTERISTICS : CANN

- Aromatic hetero ring

- Non aromatic hetero ring

- No hetero ring

GROUP TRANSFERRING CO ENZYMES : Please Broad CAST

- Pyridoxal phosphate

- Biotin

- CoA

- ATP and its relatives

- Sugar phosphates

- Thiamine pyrophosphate

ENZYMES LOCATION IN CELL

CYTOPLASM : GF / FG

- Glycolysis

- Glycogenolysis

- Glycogenesis

- Fatty Acid Synthesis

MITOCHONDRIA : O CUBE

- Oxidative Phosphorylation

- Citric Acid Cycle

- Urea Cycle

- Betaoxidation

- Electron Transport Chain

MICROSOMES : PH

- Protein Synthesis

- Hydroxylation

NUCLEI : RNH

- RNA Synthesis

- NAD Synthesis

- Histone Synthesis

METABOLISM SITES : HUG IN BOTH CYTOPLASM AND MITOCHONDRIA

- Heme Synthesis

- Urea Cycle

- Gluconeogenesis

OXIDASES : U CLAMP

- Uricase

- Cytochrome Oxidase

- Laccase

- Ascorbic Oxidase

- Monoamine Oxidase

- Phenolase

AEROBIC DEHYDROGENASE : XD LAG / X GLAD / GLADX

- Xanthine Dehydrogenase

- D –amino Acid Dehydrogenase

- L –amino Acid Dehydrogenase

- Aldehyde Dehydrogenase

- Glucose Oxidase

CYTOCHROME P45O : PROPERTIES : BHIM SLIM PHC

- **B**road **S**ubstrate **S**pecificity

- **H**aemoproteins

- **I**ntroduction of one atom of oxygen into the substrate and one into water

- **M**etabolism of many xenobiotics and steroids

- **S**mooth endoplasmic reticulum or in mitochondria

- **L**arge amounts in liver , found in most tissues

- **I**nducible (many)

- **M**olecular mass about 55KDa

- **P**olymorphism (some)

- **H**ydroxylated products are more water soluble

- **C**arcinogenic products in some cases

COENZYME Q (UBIQUINONE) : MASC

- **M**itochondria Oxidized quinone form - Aerobic Conditions

- Reduced quinol form - Anaerobic Conditions

- **A**dditional carrier present in respiratory chain linking flavoprotein to

- Cytochrome b

- **S**tructure very similar to vitamin K and vitamin E

- **C**onstituent of mitochondrial lipids

MUSCLE TISSUE

MUSCLE TISSUES IN THE BODY : CNS

- Cardiac muscle

- Non – striated muscle

- Striated muscle

MUSCLE PROTEINS : MATT

- Myosin

- Actin

- Tropomyosin

- Troponin

MYOSIN : PROPERTIES : MAGICS

- Molecular weight 5,00,000 - 2 major chains and 4 light chains

- Myosin molecules (3) with actin molecule (1) forms actomyosin

- Meromyosin (heavy) is a rod shaped protein

- ATPase activity

- Globulin

- Insoluble in water

- Cleavage by trypsin forms 2 components - meromyosins

- Soluble in dilute salt solutions

CELL MOTILITY AND CYTOSKELETON : IAM

- Intermediate Filaments

- Actin Filaments

- Microtubules

MICROTUBULES : MICA

- Mitotic Spindle

- Cilia and Flagella

- Axons and Dendrite

ROLE OF NITRIC OXIDE : Very Nice PRIL

- Vasodilator and regulator of blood pressure

- Neurotransmitter in brain and peripheral autonomic nervous system

- Neurotoxicity

- Penile Erection

- Part of primitive immune system

- Relaxation of skeletal muscle

- Inhibits adhesion , activation and aggregation of platelets

- Long - term potentiation

- Low level causes pyrolospasm in infantile hypertrophic pyloric stenosis

VITAMINS

FAT SOLUBLE VITAMINS : COMMON PROPERTIES : BHANG

- Bile salts and fats are essential for their absorption

- Have isoprene derivatives

- Apolar, hydrophobic molecules

- Normally, not excreted in urine

- Generally stored in liver

FAT SOLUBLE VITAMINS : ADEK

- A

- D

- E

- K

WATER SOLUBLE VITAMINS : COMMON PROPERTIES : SENT

- Soluble in water

- Easily absorbed

- Not stored in body (Except B12)

- Threshold for urinary excretion

VITAMIN A : RHODOPSIN VITAMIN A CYCLE : BALU MET A RHODOPSIN AT RETINA

- *B*Athorhodopsin

- Lumirhodopsin

- METArhodopsin I

- METArhodopsin II

- All – Trans - Retinal

VITAMIN A : PHYSIOLOGIC FUNCTIONS : V Might PASs

- Vision

- Maintaining (helps in) the integrity of epithelial tissues

- Preservation of structural integrity and normal permeability of cell membrane

- Accelerates normal formation of bones and teeth

- Synthesis of chrondoitin sulphate

VITAMIN D : PHYSIOLOGIC FUNCTIONS : IIST BDS / SIT BDS

- Intestinal absorption of calcium and phosphate

- Increases excretion of phosphate by kidney

- Increases citrate level of blood , bone , kidney and heart tissues

- STimulates the transcription of mRNA for calcium binding protein

- Bone mineralization

- Decreases the pH in the lower intestinal tract

- Development and growth of bone

- Simulates the activity of phytase

DEFICIENCY OF VITAMIN D : CAUSES : GASTRIC ACID

- GASTRointestinal disorder

- Anticonvulsant drugs (prolonged treatment with)

- Chronic obstructive jaundice

- Insufficient exposure to light

- Dietary insufficiency

VITAMIN E : PHYSIOLOGIC FUNCTIONS : FASt PHD

- Free radical removal

- Antioxidant action

- Selenium and vitamin E act synergestically

- Prevents

    - Peroxidative changes in membranes of mitochondria

    - Hepatic necrosis produced by lack of S containing amino acids in dietary proteins

    - Development of cerebral disorder

VITAMIN E : DEFICIENCY MANIFESTATIONS : MY NAME IS FIDHA

- Muscular dystrophy

- Neurologic disorder

- Nocturnal muscle cramp

- Increased susceptibility of erythrocytes to haemolysis by H_2O_2

- Skin changes, anaemia and oedema in infants when fed unsaturated oils.

- Fibrocytic breast disease and atherosclerosis

- Increased oxygen consumption by skeletal muscle

- Decreased erythrocyte life span

- Haemolysis, creatinuria

- Hepatic necrosis

- Anaemia occurring in pregnant and lactating women

VITAMIN K : PHYSIOLOGIC FUNCTIONS : CARE Me

- Catalyses the synthesis of prothrombin by liver

- Cofactor of carboxylase

- Antidote to poisoning by dicoumarol – type drugs

- Absorption of fat

- Reduces prothrombin time

- Regulates synthesis of clotting factors (II , VII , IX and X)

- Essential component of phosphorylation processes involved in photosynthesis in green plants

- Maintenance of normal levels of blood clotting factors

VITAMIN C : PHYSIOLOGICAL FUNCTIONS : FOM CHINA

- Formation of norepinephrine

- Oxidation – reduction reactions of the cell

- Metabolism of tyrosine and phenylalanine and also in tryptophan

- Conversion of folic acid to folinic acid (citrovorum factor)

- Hydroxylation of steroids in the adrenal cortex

- Inhibitory effect on hyaluronidase - hyaluronic acid system

- Normal regulation of colloidal condition of intercellular substances

- Absorption of iron and incorporation of plasma iron to ferritin

SCURVY : SYMPTOMS : AGE PILSS

- Anaemia

- General weakness

- Easy fracturability of bones

- Poor healing of wounds

- Internal haemorrhages

- Loosening of teeth

- Swelling of long bones

- Swelling , sponginess , tenderness and bleeding of gums

- Susceptibility to infections

THIAMINE B1 : PROPERTIES : ROADS

- Readily soluble in water

- Oxidized with potassium ferricyanide in alkaline solution

- Autoclaved at 120 degrees for 30 minutes (destroyed)

- Destroyed even at room temperature in an alkaline medium

- Dissolved in sodium bisulphate solution at pH 4.8 to 5 it is cleaved into pyrimidine half and thiazole half

- Stable in acid medium

THIAMINE : METABOLIC ROLE AS COENZYME : MAL TOP / TOP MAL

- Mitochondrial branched chain alpha keto acid decarboxylase

- ALpha ketoglutarate dehydrogenase complex

- Transketolase

- Tryptophan metabolism for the activity of enzyme tryptophan pyrrolase

- Oxydative decarboxylation (TPP)

- Pyruvate dehydrogenase complex

RIBOFLAVIN B2 : METABOLIC ROLE : CAR / RAO

- Coenzyme for enzyme catalyze oxidation – reduction reaction

- Aerobic dehydrogenase (component of)

- Respiratory chain component

RIBOFLAVIN B2 : DEFICIENCY MANIFESTATIONS : LIPS CHEST

- LIPS - redness and shiny appearance of lips

- CHeilosis

- Eyes - corneal vascularisation and inflammation

- Seborrheic dermatitis

- Tongue - painful glossitis, red purple (magenta) tongue

PYRIDOXINE B6 : COENZYME ACTIVITIES : BDS AT DCI . COM

- Brain metabolism - Formation of serotonin , GABA and catecholamines

- Desulphuration

- Synthesis of coenzyme A from pantothenic acid

- Aminoacid absorption from intestine

- Alpha amino levulunic acid synthesis

- Transulfuration reaction

- Deaminases (dehydrases)

- Codecarboxylase

- Immune response

- Cotransaminase, Kynureninase

- Oxalate metabolism

- Muscle phosphorylase

PYRIDOXINE B6 : DEFICIENCY SYMPTOMS :
ILL ALCOHOLIC

- Irritability and depression

- Infants on inadequate milk formulas

- Infants whose mothers deficient of vitamin due to long use
  of OCPs

- INH and Hydralazine act as B6 antagonist causing
  deficiency symptoms

- Inborn errors of metabolism including cystathionuria ,
  familial xanthurenic aciduria

- Alcoholics may also be deficient due to metabolism of
  ethanol to acetaldehyde

PANTOTHENIC ACID : DEFICIENCY
SYMPTOMS : FABIN GV

- Fatty Liver

- Failure In Gaining Weights

- Anaemia

- Burning Foot Syndrome

- Irritability

- Inadequate Growth

- Nausea

- Gastrointestinal Disorders

- Vomiting

RICKETS : SYMPTOMS : RBC

- Rickety rosary - Beading at costochondral junctions of ribs

- Renal ricket caused by defective transport of phosphate by renal tubules

- Bone deformities

- Bossing - Pigeon chest

- Bones soft due to non deposition of calcium salts

- Bones bent easily

- Craniotabes – small round unossified areas in membranous bones of skull

VITAMIN B3 (NIACIN) DEFICIENCY : 3D's PELLAGRA

- Dermatitis

- Dementia

- Diarrhea

PORPHYRIAS : ACUTE INTERMITTENT PORPHYRIA : SYMPTOMS : 5 P s

- Pain in abdomen

- Polyneuropathy

- Psychological abnormalities

- Pink urine

- Precipitated by drugs (eg Barbiturates, Oral Contraceptives, Sulpha drugs)

GLYCOGEN STORAGE : ENZYME DEFECT : ABCD

- Anderson's - Branching Enzyme

- Cori's - Debranching Enzyme

METABOLIC ACIDOSIS (NORMAL ANION GAP): CAUSES

WITH HYPERKALEMIA : RAISE K+

- RTA type 4

- Aldosterone or Mineralocorticoid Deficiency

- Iatrogenic : NH4CL, HCL

- Stenosis : Obstructive Uropathy

- Early Uremia

WITH HYPOKALEMIA : REDUCE K+

- Renal TA type 1 and 2

- Diarrhoea

- Urine diversion into gut

- Carbomic anhydrase inhibitor
  Ex – hyperventilation

CITRIC ACID CYCLE

CITRIC ACID CYCLE : COMPONENTS : Oh Citric Acid Is Ofcourse A Silly Stupid Funny Molecule

- Oxaloacetate

- Citrate

- Aconitate

- Isocitrate

- Oxalosuccinate

- Alpha Keto Glutarate

- Succinyl CoA

- Succinate

- Fumarate

- Malate

CITRIC ACID CYCLE : NADH FORMING STEPS : IAM NADH

- Isocitrate → Alpha Keto Glutarate

- Alpha Keto Glutarate → Succinyl CoA

- Malate → Oxaloacetate

CITRIC ACID CYCLE : FADH FORMING STEP : FFFF / 4 F S

- FADH Formed in Fumarate Forming Step

- Succinate → Fumarate

FOLATE DEFICIENCY CAUSES : A FOLIC DROP

- Alcoholism
- Folic Acid Antagonists
- Oral Contraceptives
- Low Dietary Intake
- Infection with Giardia
- Celiac Sprue
- Dilantin
- Relative Folate Deficiency
- Old
- Pregnancy

MITOCHONDRIAL DNA : mt DNA : MT

- Maternal Transfer
- Mutates Tremendously

GLYCOGEN STORAGE DISEASE : TYPES I – VI

- Von Gierke's
- Pompe's
- Cori's
- Anderson's
- Mc Ardle's
- Her's

[SI]CKLE CELL DISEASE : [SI]

- Sixth amino acid substitution of Beta chain

- Van den Bergh reaction (Jaundice Test) : IUCD

- Indirect : Unconjugated bilirubin (I and U are vowels)

- Direct : Conjugated bilirubin

HAEMOGLOBIN BINDING CURVE : CAUSES OF SHIFT TO RIGHT : EXCERCISING MUSCLE

- Exercise

- Increased CO_2

- Lactic Acid

- 2, 3 BPG

- Temperature

ADRENALINE MECHANISM : ABC

- Adrenaline Activates

- Beta Receptors Increases

- Cyclic AMP

CARBON MONOXIDE : ELECTRON TRANSPORT CHAIN TARGET : CO

- CO blocks Cytochrome Oxidase

ETC COMPLEX IV : CC

- CO

- CN

DICARBOXYLIC ACIDS : Oh My Son Go And Play SuAS

- Oxalic Acid

- Malonic Acid

- Succinic Acid

- Glutaric Acid

- Adipic Acid

- Pimelic Acid

- Suberic Acid

- Azelaic Acid

- Sebacic Acid

INFANTILE BERIBERI SYMPTOMS : Great BERI'S

- Great Heartedness (dilated heart)

- Breathlessness

- Eatlessness (Anorexia)

- Restlessness

- Insomnia (Sleepnessness)

- Soundlessness (Aphonia)

ACETYL CoA AND ACETOACETYL CoA : AMINOACIDS FORMING THEM : Tryp ILL

- Tryptophan

- Isoleucine

- Leucine

- Lysine

FABRY'S DISEASE : FABRY'S

- Foam cells found in glomeruli and tubules / Febrile episodes

- Alpha galactosidase A deficiency/Angiokeratomas

- Burning pain in extremities / BUN increased in serum/Boys

- Renal failure

- YX genotype (male, X linked recessive)

- Sphingolipidoses

ETC : ROTEN[ONE]'S SITE OF ACTION

- Site specific inhibitor of complex ONE

TYPE ONE GLYCOGEN STORAGE DISEASE : VON

- Von Giereke's disease

PYRUVATE : PRODUCTS OF COMPLETE OXIDATION : 432(1)

- 4 NADH

- 3 CO2

- 2 (1)   = 1 FADH + 1 GTP

INSULIN FUNCTION : PG INSIDE / GP INSIDE

- Potassium and Glucose into cells

COLLAGEN : COLLAGEN

- C - terminal propeptide (procollagen) / Covalent Cross links / C vitamin / Connective tissue / Cartilage / Chondroblasts / Copper cofactor (Covalent Cross linking)

- Outside the cell is where collagen normally functions / Osteoblasts / Osteogenesis imperfect

- Lysyl hydroxylase / Lysyl oxidase (Oxidatively deaminates lysyl and hydroxylysyl residues to form collagen cross links, last biosynthesis step)

- Long triple helical fibres / Ligaments

- Alpha chains / Attached by H bonds form triple helix / Ascorbate for hydroxylation of lysyl and prolyl residues of pro - Alpha chains (post translational modification)

- Gly in every third position / Glycosylation of hydroxyl group of hydroxylysine with Glucose and Galactose ; Golgi allows procallagen to Go outside of the cell

- Extracellular matrix / Eye (cornea, sclera) / Ehlers - Danlos syndrome

- N - terminal propeptide (procollagen) / Nonhelical terminal extensions

HYPERVITAMINOSIS A : SIGNS AND SYMPTOMS : HARD

- Headache / Hepatomegaly

- Anorexia / Alopecia

- Really Painful Bones

- Dry Skin / Drowsiness

[PH]ENYL KETONURIA : ENZYME DEFICIENT : PH

- Phenylalanine Hydroxylase

PROTEIN SYNTHESIS

- [E]xons : [E]

- [E]xpressed

- [I]ntrons : [I]

- [I]ntruders

ORAL HISTOLOGY
AND
DENTAL ANATOMY

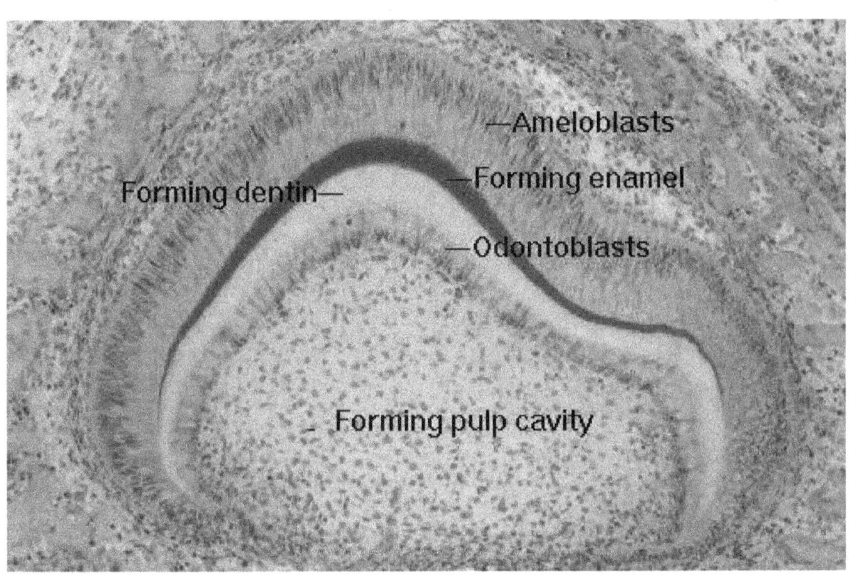

ORAL HISTOLOGY

DEVELOPMENT AND GROWTH OF TEETH

DEVELOPING TOOTH : STAGES OF ENAMEL ORGAN : BCB

- Bud

- Cap

- Bell

DENTAL PAPILLA FORMS DP

D and P are the first letters of words Dental Papilla

- Dentin

- Pulp

DENTAL SAC : PDC (Pre Degree Course)

- Periodontal Ligament

- Cementum

MESODERM : DENTAL SAC : PLACE

- Periodontal Ligament

- Alveolar bone

- CEmentum

TOOTH FORMATION : STAGES : IHMA

- Initiation

- Histodifferentiation

- Morphodifferentiation

- Apposition

ENAMEL EPITHELIUM

- In{n}er - Colum{n}ar

- Outer - Cuboidal

ENAMEL

ENAMEL : AEO (All vowels)

- Ameloblasts - Formative Cells

- Avascular

- Ectodermal Origin

- Epithelial Tissue

- Odontoclasts - Degenerative Cells

ENAMEL : EEE

- Ectodermal Origin

- Epithelial Tissue

ENAMEL PROTEINS : A SEAT

- Amelogenins 90%

- Enamelin (Sheathelin)

- Tuftelin

- Amelin

HUNTER – SCHREGER BANDS (HSB) : CALORIE SPA

- Change in direction of enamel rods is responsible for HSB

- Alternate dark and light bands

- Longitudinal ground sections (best seen in) under

- Oblique reflected light

- ORIginate at Dentinoenamel border and pass outward

- Enamel crystals aggregate in each zone of HSB deviated

- Slightly different permeability and different content of organic material

- Prisms cut longitudinally to produce dark bands - Parazones

- Prisms cut [T]ranseversely to produce [L]ight bands - [D]iazones (remember [TLD] film badges)

- Angle between Parazones and diazones is about 40 degrees

INCREMENTAL LINES OF RETZIUS : ABCDE PRIL O TOM

- About 25 - 30 do not reach surface

- Brownish bands in ground sections of the enamel

- Cervical(in) part of crown, they run obliquely

- DEJ to surface they deviate occlusally

- Evenly spaced striae of Retzius represent a 6 - 11 day rhythm in enamel formation

- Periodic bending of enamel rods to variations in basic organic structure or to a physiologic calcification rythym

- Reflect Variations in structure and mineralization - hypomineralisaion / hypermineralisation

- ILLustrate incremental pattern of enamel, ie, successive apposition of layers of enamel during formation of the crown

- LOngitudinal section, they surround the tip of the dentin

- Transverse section of tooth, appear as concentric circles

- Other Retzius lines are suggested due to stress

- Mean daily rate of formation about 3.5 microns increases from inner to outer enamel

- Moderate intensity considered normal

- Metabolic disturbances can upset rhythmic alterations

SURFACE STRUCTURES : PEN

- Prismless Enamel

- Perikymata

- Pits

- Enamel Caps

- Enamel Brochs

- Neonatal line or neonatal ring

ENAMEL CUTICLE : PEN DATE

- Primary Enamel Cuticle

- Nasmyth Membrane

- Delicate Membrane

- Ameloblasts

- Typical Basal Lamina

- Enamel Cuticle

ENAMEL LAMELLA : THIN LED CD

- Thin

- Leaflike structures

- Longitudinal and Radial directions (extend in)

- Extend (may) to Dentin

- Consists of organic material

- Confused with cracks in ground sections

- Careful Decalcification, Cracks Disappear Enamel lamellae persist

- Caries producing bacteria - road of entry to initiate caries

- Develop in planes of tension

ENAMEL LAMELLA : TYPES : ABCD

- A - Calcified (poorly) Calcified Rod Segments

- B - Degenerated Cells

- C - Deciduous Teeth

- ACE   ABCD

- A - Confined (Restricted) to Enamel

- BC - Dentin (May reach into)

DENTINOENAMEL JUNCTION : SOM CDE

- Scalloped Line

- Occlusal Area (more pronounced in)

- Masticatory Stress (Greater)

- Convexities Directed to Dentin

- Crystals of Dentin and

- Enamel mix each other

AGE CHANGES : AGE CD CD

- Attrition

- GEneralised loss of rod ends and perikymata

- Crystal size increases due to ions acquired from oral fluids

- Decreases the pores between them

- Decrease (reduction) in permeability

- Caries resistance may be increased

- Darker teeth

DEVELOPMENT : EPITHELIAL ENAMEL ORGAN : O ISC

- Outer Enamel Epithelium

- Inner Enamel Epithelium

- Stellate Reticulum

- Stratum Intermedium

- Cervical Loop

CYCLE OF AMELOBLAST

MOF MPD (My Old Friends Made Programme to Delhi)

- Morphogenic

- Organising

- Formative

- Maturative

- Protective

- Desmolytic

MDS MP / MIS MP

- Morphogenetic Stage

- Differentiation Stage / Inductive Stage

- Secretory Stage

- Maturation Stage

- Protective Stage

AMELOGENESIS : ETAM

- Enamel Matrix Formation

- Tome's Process Development

- Ameloblasts Covering Maturing Enamel

- Mineralisation and Maturation of Enamel Matrix

DENTIN

TYPES OF DENTIN : PCM ISRO

- Predentin

- Peritubular Dentin

- Circumpulpal Dentin

- Mantle Dentin

- Intertubular Dentin

- Interglobular Dentin

- Secondary Dentin / Adventitious Dentin

- Sclerotic / Transparent Dentin

- Reparative Dentin / Tertiary Dentin / Response Dentin

- Osteodentin

PRIMARY DENTIN :

MANTLE DENTIN : OMFS PER LAST VON

- Outer or most peripheral part of dentin

- Mainly type III collagen

- Matrix vesicles are involved in mineralization of mantle dentin

- First formed dentin

- Fewer defects than circumpulpal dentin

- Soft - cushioning effect to the teeth

- Perpendicular to DEJ fibrils are formed

- Larger collagen fibrils than are present in circumpulpal dentin

- Less mineralised

- Argyrophilic

- Silver stained - von Korff's fibres

- Twenty micrometer thick

- VONkorff's fibres - large diameter collagen fibres

CIRCUMPULPAL DENTIN : BSC MAths

- Bulk of tooth

- Smaller in diameter collagen fibrils

- Closely packed collagen fibrils

- More mineral than mantle dentin

- All of dentin formed before root completion

SECONDARY DENTIN : Not FRAD

- Narrow band of dentin bordering the pulp

- Not formed in response to any external stimuli

- Not formed uniformly and

- Fewer tubules than primary dentin

- Regular arrangement of dentinal tubules - Regular secondary dentin

- Appears greater amounts on roof and floor of the coronal pulp chamber

- Dentin formed after root completion

TERTIARY DENTIN : RRR

- Reparative Dentin

- Reactionary Dentin

- Regenerated Dentin

DEAD TRACTS : D

- Appear (D)ark in (T)ransmitted light

- White in Reflected light

AGE AND FUNCTIONAL CHANGES : VIT D REST

- VITality of Dentin

- Dead Tracts

- Reparative Dentin

- Sclerotic / Transparent Dentin

SCLEROTIC OR TRANSPARENT DENTIN : ACE STIMULI CAUSE HANDCRAFT TEMP

- Attrition

- Abrasion

- Cavity Preparation

- Erosion STIMULI

- CAUSE collagen fibres and apatite crystals to begin appearing in the dentinal tubules

- HArder than Normal Dentin

- Crystals smaller than those present in normal dentin

- Refractive indices in occluded dentinal tubules are equalized - transparent

- Reflected light - Dark

- Aging hardness greater than those below carious lesions

- Fracture toughness reduced

- Transmitted light

- Transparent or light

- Elastic properties not altered

- Elastic modulus almost similar to that of intertubular, peritubular and healthy dentin

- Mineral density greater

- Prolong vitality (reduced permeability)

THEORIES OF PAIN TRANSMISSION IN DENTIN : DTH

- Direct Neural Stimulation

- Transduction Theory

- Hydrodynamic Theory

ORDER OF SENSITIVITY DURING CAVITY PREPARATION : PD DPC

- Pulp

- Dentino Enamel Junction (DEJ)

- Deep Layers of Dentin near Pulp

- Cementum

MATRIX VESICLES : MMMW

- Involved in Mineralisation of Mantle Dentin and Woven bone

PULP

STRUCTURAL FEATURES : SPECIALISED ODONTOGENIC REGION : OCC

- Odontoblasts (dentin forming cells)

- Cell Free Zone (Weil's Zone)

- Cell Rich Zone

DEFENSE CELLS : MAM PHD / PHD MAM

- MAcrophages

- Mast Cells

- Plasma Cells

- Histiocytes

- Dendritic Cells

FUNCTIONS OF PULP : FPD NRI / INF RPD

- Formative

- Protective

- Defensive

- Nutritive

- Reparative

- Inductive

ZONES OF PULP

- Cell free zone(Weil's zone)

- Cell rich zone

REGRESSIVE CHANGES (AGING) : CV in PDF format

- Cell Changes

- Vascular Changes

- Pulp Stones / Denticles

- Diffuse Calcifications

- Fibrosis

PULP STONES / DENTICLES – CLASSIFICATION: DIFALT

- DIffuse

- FAlse

- True

CEMENTUM

CEMENTUM : CCC

- Connective Tissue

- Cementoblasts – Formative Cells

CEMENTUM : FUNCTIONS : CAAR

- Anchorage

- Adaptation

- Repair

PERIODONTAL LIGAMENT

PERIODONTIUM : PERIODONTAL LIGAMENT ABCD

- Periodontal Ligament

- Alveolar Bone

- Cementum

- Dentogingival Junction

PERIODONTIUM : ATTACHMENTS : ABCD

- Alveolar Bone to the

- Bone of the jaws

- Cementum to the

- Dentin of the root of the tooth

TISSUE HOMEOSTASIS : CYTOKINES : MFP IIT / PFM ITI

- Matrix Metallo Poteinases and their tissue inhibitors (MMPs)

- Fibroblast Growth Factor (FGF)

- Platelet Derived Growth Factor (PDGF)

- Interleukin - 1 (IL - 1)

- Interferon Gamma

- Transforming Growth Factor (TGF)

PERIODONTAL LIGAMENT : CELLS : SPRED / DEPRES / PRESED

- Synthetic cells : **COF**

  - Cementoblasts

  - Osteoblasts

  - Fibroblasts

- Progenitor cells

- Resorptive cells : **COF**

  - Cementoclasts

  - Osteoclasts

  - Fibroblasts

- Epithelial cells

  - Epithelial rests of Malassez

- Defense cells : **DME**

  - Mast cells

  - Macrophages

  - Eosinophils

EXTRACELLULAR SUBSTANCE : EFGs

- Fibres : **O RICES**

- Oxytalan

- Reticular

- Indifferent Fibre Plexus

- Collagen

- Elastic
- Secondary
- Ground Substance : **PG**
- Proteoglycans
- Glycoproteins

PERIODONTAL LIGAMENT : COLLAGEN FIBRES : O HITA

- Oblique
- Horizontal
- Inter Radicular
- Trans Septal
- Alveolar Crest
- Apical

PERIODONTAL LIGAMENT : FUNCTIONS : HENS

- Homeostatic
- Eruptive
- Nutritive
- Supportive
- Sensory

[E]P[IT]HELIAL CELLS : [E] [TI]

- K[E]ra[TI]n

NER[V]E : [V]

- [V]imentin

[M]u[S]cle : [M] [S]

- De[S][M]in

BONE

CLASSIFICATION : BASED ON : MDS

BASED ON MICROSCOPIC STRUCTURE : ICC

- Immature / woven Bone
- Compact / Cortical Bone
- Cancellous / Spongy Bone

BASED ON DEVELOPMENT : EI

- Endochondral Bones
- Intramembranous Bones

BASED ON SHAPE : FILLS

- Flat Bones
- Irregular Bones
- Long Bones
- Short Bones
- Sesamoid Bones

COMPOSITION OF BONE : NON COLLAGENOUS PROTEINS :

ABCD PLOT VIP FM

- Alkaline phosphatase
- Alpha 2Hs Glycoproteins
- Bone Sialoprotein

- Bone Morphogenetic Proteins (BMPs)
- Biglycan (Chondroitin Sulfate Proteoglycan I)
- Cytokines
- Decorin (Chondroitin Sulfate Proteoglycan II)
- Proteoglycans
- Procollagen Peptides
- Proteases
- Protease Inhibitors
- Lysyl Oxidase
- Osteocalcin
- Osteopontin
- Osteonectin
- TRAMP / Dermatopontin
- Thrombospondin
- Vitronectin
- Insulin like Growth Factors
- Platelet Derived Growth Factors
- Fibroblast Growth Factor
- Fibronectin
- Matrix Gla Protein

ORAL MUCOUS MEMBRANE

FUNCTIONS OF ORAL MUCOSA : PROSECute

- PROtection

- SEnsation

- SECretion

ORAL MUCOSA : CLASSIFICATION BASED ON FUNCTIONAL CRITERIA : LMS

- Lining or Reflecting Mucosa

- Masticatory Mucosa

- Specialised Mucosa

KERATINISED EPITHELIUM : CELL LAYERS : BSGC

- Basale

- Spinosum

- Granulosum

- Corneum

KERATINOCYTES AND NON KERATINOCYTES : KLMN

- Keratinocytes

- Langerhans Cell ,

- Melanocytes and

- Merkel Cell are

- Non Keratinocytes

ORAL MUCOSA : CELLS : KMML [Kerala Minerals and Metals Limited]

- Keratinocytes

- Non Keratinocytes

  - Melanocytes

  - Merkel cells

  - Langerhans Cells

NON KERATINISED EPITHELIUM : LAYERS : BIS

- Basale

- Intermedium

- Superficiale

KERATINISED AREAS : GH [General Hospital]

- Gingiva

- Hard palate

GINGIVAL LIGAMENT : C DAS / CD DAS

- Circular group

- Dentogingival Group

- Dentoperiosteal Group

- Alveologingival Group

- Supracrestal or Transseptal Fibres

TASTE BUDS : PRESENT ON : PC FOLDS FUNGIFORM PAPILLAE

- Posterior Surface of Epiglottis

- Circumvallate Papilla – (on inner wall of trough surrounding)

- FOLDs of FOLiate Papillae

- Fu[NG]iform papillae (some) at the tip and lateral borders of to[NG]ue

SALIVARY GLANDS

PAROTID GLAND : SSS

- Serous (Purely)

- Stenson's duct

- Second molar (maxillary) - Opens near the maxillary 2nd molar in the buccal mucosa

SEROUS CELLS : AGE

- Acid Phosphatases

- Glucuronidase

- Glucosidase

- Galactosidase

- Esterases

MYOEPITHELIAL CELLS : DISC

- Ductal pressure measurement after appropriate stimulation indicates a contractile process.

- Immunofluorescent studies indicate presence of myosin, actin and related proteins.

- Structure similar to that of smooth muscles.

- Cinemicrography of individual secretory stimulated to secrete in vivo reveal a regular pulsatile movement of entire unit.

MYOEPITHELIAL CELLS : FUNCTIONS : RASH

- Reduce Luminal Volume

- Accelerate initial outflow of saliva from acini.

- Secretory pressure (contribute to) in acini or duct.

- Support underlying parenchyma and reduce back permeation of fluid.

- Help salivary flow to overcome increase in peripheral resistance of the ducts.

MINOR SALIVARY GLANDS : LPG VON

- Labial and Buccal Glands

- Lingual Glands

- Palatine Glands

- Glossopalatine Glands

- VON Ebner Glands

SALIVA : CONSTITUENTS : CM LPG BAG

- Calcium

- Maltose

- Lipase

- Phosphate

- Gustin

- Bicarbonate

- Amylase

- Glycoprotein and Water

ANTIBACTERIAL : LIP

- Lactoferrin
- Lysozyme
- IgA
- Peroxidase

FUNCTIONS OF SALIVA : DPM TEST

- Digestion
- Protection of oral cavity and oral environment
- Mastication and Deglutition
- Taste Perception
- Excretion
- Speech
- Tissue repair

TOOTH ERUPTION : THEORIES : HR BP

- Hydrostatic Pressure
- Root Formation
- Bone Remodelling
- Periodontal Ligament Theory / Hammock Ligament Theory

DENTAL ANATOMY

TOOTH NOTATION : PUFs

- Palmar

- Universal

- FDI

ERUPTION TIME – PERMANENT DENTITION

- 6 - 7   7 - 8   7 - 8   8 - 9 (6 - 9)

- 9 - 10   11 - 12 (9 - 12)

- 10 - 11   10 - 12 (10 - 11; 12)

- 10 - 12   11 - 12 (10 ; 11 - 12)

- 6   6

DENTITION

- Primary : 6 months - 6 years

- Mixed : 6 years -12 years

- Permanent : 12 years onwards

ERUPTION SEQUENCE

- Permanent Maxillary Dentition : 6-1-2-4-3-5-7-8 OR

- Permanent Maxillary Dentition : 6-1-2-4-5-3-7-8

- Permanent Mandibular Dentition : 6-1-2-3-4-5-7-8 (12345 and 78 in the order)

FUNCTIONAL CUSPS : CSF

- Centric – Holding Cusps

- Stamp Cusps

NON FUNCTIONAL CUSPS : BULL

- Buccal of Upper and

- Lingual of Lower

- OVER JET : HORIZONTAL OVERLAP

- OVER B[IT]E : VER[TI]CAL OVERLAP

TEETH RELATIONS IN OCCLUSION : S RCC

- Surface Contact

- Ridge - Sulcus Contact

- Cusp - Embrasure Contact

- Cusp - Fossa Contact

CURVATURES OF OCCLUSAL PLANE : MONSON and WILSON find PLEASURE on REVERSE SPEEd

- Monson's Curve

- Wilson's Curve

- Pleasure Curve

- Reverse Curve

- Spee (Curve of)

OCCLUSION : BCG MUTUALLY PROTECTS

- Balanced Occlusion - in complete dentures
- Canine Guided Occlusion
- Group Function Occlusion
- MUTUALLY PROTECTed Occlusion

LIGAMENTS OF TMJ : CAPTain Styphen

- CAPsular Ligament
- Temporomandibular Ligament
- Stylomandibular Ligament
- Sphenomandibular Ligament

MUSCLES OF MASTICATION : M MLT

- Masseter
- Medial Pterygoid
- Lateral Pterygoid
- Temporalis
- LINE ANGLES : 8 11 6 11   8 (PALINDROMIC)
- POINT ANGLES : 4 6 3 6 4 (SAME READING FROM BOTH SIDES)

CORNE[R ST]ONE OF DENTAL ARCH : [RST]

- MAXILLARY FI[RST] MOLAR
- CORNER TOOTH OF DENTAL ARCH : MAXILLARY CANINE

BUTLER'S FIELD THEORY : HUMAN DENTITION : MCI

- Molariform

- Canine Region

- Incisor Region